The Art of Living

A Guide to Contentment, Joy, and Fulfillment

Above, Pilgrims and prayer wheels blur as the pilgrims perform a "kora" or circumambulation of Tashikhyil Monastery, Amdo, Eastern Tibet.

The Art of Living

A Guide to Contentment, Joy, and Fulfillment

His Holiness the XIV Dalai Lama
Translated by Geshe Thupten Jinpa

Photographs by Ian Cumming

GRAMERCY BOOKS
NEW YORK

Also by His Holiness the Dalai Lama:
A Simple Path
Transforming the Mind

This 2005 edition is published by Gramercy Books,
an imprint of Random House Value Publishing,
a division of Random House, Inc., New York,
by arrangement with Thorsons,
an imprint of HarperCollins*Publishers*, London.

Gramercy is a registered trademark and the colophon
is a trademark of Random House, Inc.

Random House
New York • Toronto • London • Sydney • Auckland
www.randomhouse.com

Printed and bound in Thailand by
Imago

A catalog record for this title is available
from the Library of Congress.

ISBN 0-517-22630-8

1 3 5 7 9 10 8 6 4 2

Contents

Above, His Holiness the Fourteenth Dalai Lama in front of a Tibetan national flag at a press conference in London, May 1998.

Preface

His Holiness the Dalai Lama is the head of state and spiritual leader of the Tibetan people. He is also regarded as the world's foremost Buddhist leader and the manifestation of Chenrezig, the Bodhisattva of Compassion.

A scholar and a man of peace, His Holiness the Dalai Lama has traveled the world, not only to raise international awareness of the enormous suffering of the Tibetan people, but also to talk about Buddhism and the power of compassion.

Since 1959 His Holiness has been living in exile in Dharamsala, India, after China's troops crushed a Tibetan National Uprising against Chinese rule in Tibet. China invaded Tibet in 1949-50.

In 1989 His Holiness was awarded the Nobel Peace Prize for his non-violent struggle for the liberation of Tibet. Since coming into exile he has met many of the world's political and spiritual leaders. He has shared with these leaders his views on human interdependence and his concerns about the arms trade, threats to the environment, and intolerance.

His Holiness describes himself as a simple Buddhist monk. In lectures and tours, he disarms audiences with his simplicity, humor, and great warmth. Everywhere his message is the same – the importance of love, compassion, and forgiveness.

The text for this book is taken from a series of public lectures given by His Holiness the Dalai Lama at Wembley Conference Centre in London, England, in May 1993. The Office of Tibet is therefore delighted to be able to offer these words of His Holiness to a world-wide audience.

In the original lectures, His Holiness the Dalai Lama spoke mainly in English, but also to his official translator in Tibetan. The May 1993 visit was sponsored by The Tibet Foundation, London.

The Office of Tibet would like to thank Jane Rasch and Cait Collins for their many hours spent on transcribing the tapes. We would also like to thank His Holiness's translator, Geshe Thupten Jinpa, and Heather Wardle for their work in editing the text into book form.

– Mrs Kesang Y Takla

Former Representative of His Holiness the Dalai Lama, London.

Contentment,
Joy, and
Living Well

Left, His Holiness the Dalai Lama on the balcony at the Kalachakra Initiation Ceremony,
Spiti, India, August 2000.

"The basic fact is that all sentient beings, particularly human beings, want happiness and do not want pain and suffering."

Concerned people have asked me to talk about certain subjects and about the best way to deal with the different situations of life. I will try to explain these things in such a way that ordinary people can see how to utilize their own potential in order to face unpleasant situations, such as death, and also mental frustrations, such as anger and hatred.

I am a Buddhist and my whole way of training is according to the Buddhist teaching or Buddha Dharma. Although I speak from my own experience, I feel that no one has the right to impose his or her beliefs on another person. I will not propose to you that my way is best. The decision is up to you. If you find some point which may be suitable for you, then you can carry out experiments for yourself. If you find that it is of no use, then you can discard it.

The basic fact is that all sentient beings, particularly human beings, want happiness and do not want pain and suffering. On those grounds, we have every right to be happy and to use different methods or means to overcome suffering and to achieve happier lives. These methods, however, should not infringe on the rights of others, nor should they create more suffering for others. It is worthwhile to think seriously about the positive and negative consequences of these methods. You should be aware that there are differences between short-term and long-term interests and consequences. If there is a conflict between the short-term interest and the long-term interest, the long-term interest is more important. Buddhists usually say that there is no absolute and that everything is relative. So we must judge according to the circumstances.

Left, Two monks play Tibetan shawms (gyaling) at the end of a ceremony beside a wall of Tagtsang Lhamo Monastery, Amdo, Eastern Tibet.

Our experiences and feelings are mainly related to our bodies and our minds. We know from our daily experience that mental happiness is beneficial. For instance, though two people may face the same kind of tragedy, one person may face it more easily than the other due to his or her mental attitude.

I believe that the idea that all human problems can be solved by machines or by matter is wrong. Of course, material facilities are extremely useful. At the same time, it is quite natural that all our problems cannot be solved by material facilities alone. In a material society there is just as much mental unrest and frustration, if not more. This shows us that we are human beings after all. We are not the product of machines and our bodies are different from purely mechanical things. Therefore, we must think seriously about our own inner abilities and deeper values.

I believe that if someone really wants a happy life then it is very important to pursue both internal and external means; in other words, material development and mental development. One could also say "spiritual development," but when I say "spiritual" I do not necessarily mean any kind of religious faith. When I use the word "spiritual" I mean basic human good qualities. These are: human affection, a sense of involvement, honesty, discipline, and human intelligence properly guided by good motivation. We have all these things from birth; they do not come to us later in our lives. Religious faith, however, comes later. In this regard, I believe that there are two levels to the various religious teachings. On one level, religious teachings talk about God or the Almighty, or, in Buddhism, about Nirvana and the next life. Yet on a different level, all religious teachings and traditions teach us to be good human beings, to be warm-hearted people. These religious teachings simply strengthen the basic

Right, A view of prayer flags leading up to Leh Monastery in the early evening light, Ladakh, India.

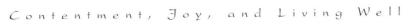

"With the realization of one's own potential and self-confidence in one's ability, one can build a better world."

human good qualities which we have from birth.

As humans, we all have the same human potential, unless there is some sort of retarded brain function. The wonderful human brain is the source of our strength and the source of our future, provided we utilize it in the right direction. If we use the brilliant human mind in the wrong way, it is really a disaster. I think human beings are the superior sentient beings on this planet. Humans have the potential not only to create happy lives for themselves, but also to help other beings. We have a natural creative quality and it is very important to realize this.

It is my belief that the human brain and basic human compassion are by nature in some kind of balance. Sometimes, when we grow up, we may neglect human affection and simply concentrate on the human brain, thus losing the balance. It is

then that disasters and unwelcome things happen. If we look at different species of mammals, we will see that nature is very important and that it is a forceful factor that creates some sort of balanced way.

With the realization of one's own potential and self-confidence in one's ability, one can build a better world. According to my own experience, self-confidence is very important. That sort of confidence is not a blind one; it is an awareness of one's own potential. On that basis, human beings can transform themselves by increasing the good qualities and reducing the negative qualities. Transformation does not mean 100 percent change. Without a basis of something to aim for, how do we develop good things? Buddhists call this potential "Buddha Nature," which is also the fundamental Clear Light nature of the mind.

Left, Monks prepare to pour the sand from the Kalachakra sand mandala into a small lake above Ki Monastery, Spiti, India.

Above, Monks at the Kalachakra Initiation Ceremony, Ki Monastery, Spiti, India.
Right, Prayer wheels spinning at Tashikhyil Monastery, Amdo, Eastern Tibet.

The fundamental teaching of the Buddha is his teaching on the Four Noble Truths: 1) That there is suffering; 2) that suffering has cause; 3) that there is cessation of suffering; and, 4) that there is a path to such freedom. The underlying principle of this teaching is the universal principle of causality. What becomes important in the understanding of this basic teaching is a genuine awareness of one's own potentials and the need to utilize them to their fullest. Seen in this light, every human action becomes significant.

For example, the smile is a very important feature of the human face. But because of human intelligence, even that good part of human nature can be used in the wrong way, such as sarcastic smiles or diplomatic smiles, which only serve to create suspicion. I feel that a genuine, affectionate smile is very important in our day-to-day lives. How one creates that smile largely depends on one's own attitude. It is illogical to expect smiles from others if one does not smile oneself. Therefore, one can see that many things depend on one's own behavior.

Now we should talk about our motivation and mental attitude. As I mentioned earlier, the facility which can provide positive things also has the potential for negative things. The important thing is to use human intelligence and judgment, and to be mindful of the benefits for long-term and short-term happiness. Up to a certain point,

the body itself is a good indicator. For instance, if some sort of food causes you discomfort one day, then later you will not want to consume that type of food. It seems that at a certain stage the body itself can tell us what is suitable for our well-being and happiness and what is not. For example, on certain days we tend to have a greater wish to eat green salads and certain vegetables, while on other days we may wish to have something else. In a way, these are bodily indications pointing out what is conducive to our constitution and what is not.

While it is very clear, for instance, that when our bodies need more liquid we develop thirst, sometimes our bodies' indications may be confusing. In those instances it is the responsibility of human intelligence to judge what is best.

Sometimes your intelligence may oppose your immediate desire because it knows the long-term consequences. Thus, the role of intelligence is to determine the positive and negative potential of an event or factor which could have both positive and negative results. It is the role of intelligence, with the full awareness that is provided by education, to judge and accordingly utilize the potential for one's own benefit or well-being.

If we examine our mental world, we find that there are various mental factors which have both positive and negative aspects. For instance, we can look at two types of mental factors which are quite similar: one is self-confidence and the other is conceit or pride. Both of them are similar in that they are uplifting states of mind which give you a certain degree of confidence and boldness. But conceit and pride tend to lead to more negative consequences, whereas self-confidence tends to lead to more positive consequences. I usually

Left, Monks walking in the hills above
Ki Monastery, Spiti, India.

"Attachment tends to lead to negative consequences, whereas love and compassion lead to positive consequences."

make a distinction between different types of ego. One type of ego is self-cherishing in order to get some benefit for itself, disregarding the rights of others and even taking advantage of others with acts such as killing, stealing, and so on. This is the negative ego. Another ego says, "I must be a good human being. I must serve. I must take full responsibility." That kind of strong feeling of "I" or self opposes some of our negative emotions. Unless you have a strong feeling of self-confidence based on a strong self, it is very difficult to do battle with these negative emotions. So there are two types of ego, and wisdom or intelligence makes a distinction. Similarly, we must be able to distinguish between genuine humility and a lack of confidence. One may confuse the two because both of these are sort of slightly humbling mental functions, but one is positive and the other is negative.

Another example of this may be seen if we examine lovingkindness and compassion on the one hand, and strong attachment on the other. While both are concerned with an object of endearment, strong attachment tends to lead to negative consequences, whereas love and compassion lead to more positive consequences. Thus two states of mind which show the same basic characteristics can have differing negative and positive results.

Desire is the same. There is both positive and negative desire. I think generally that desire which has proper reasons is positive, whereas desire which has no proper reasons is negative and can lead to problems. Desire is the prime mover in achieving happiness now and for the future. From the Buddhist viewpoint, the attainment of Buddhahood can be achieved only through a certain type of desire. For instance, the Mahayana Buddhist literature mentions two desires or two aspirations. One is the

Right, Young layman in traditional Amdo dress,
Ganja grasslands, Amdo, Eastern Tibet.

aspiration to be of benefit to all sentient beings and the other is the aspiration to attain fully the Enlightened state for that purpose. Without these two types of aspiration, the attainment of full Enlightenment is not possible. But there are also negative things which result from desire. The antidote to this negative desire is contentment. There are always extremes, but the middle way is the proper way. So if desire pushes you toward the extreme, then your intelligence has the responsibility to check that course and return you to the center.

The sense of contentment is a key factor for attaining happiness. Bodily health, material wealth, and companions and friends are three factors for happiness. Contentment is the key that will determine the outcome of your relations with all three of these factors.

First, with regard to the body, one can see that too much attachment to one's own body sometimes leads to problems. For that reason, Buddhist training looks at the body from a different angle and tries to analyze the nature of the body. To me, thinking along these lines is very useful. I think about the source of my body and the very nature of blood, bones, and flesh. The body is not something pure. Even the act of birth is bloody. Also, no matter how beautiful or polished your body appears on the outside, inside there are still a lot of dirty things. With the covering of skin, the human body sometimes looks very beautiful. But if you look more closely, then this body is really quite horrible! Even though we consume good food, with a nice color, taste, and smell, the food is transformed into dirty things. Yet if we try to remove these dirty aspects of the body we cannot survive. And this is the case not only for other people's bodies, but one's own body too. Most importantly, it is because of our bodies that we have illness, old age, pain, and death. Yet despite these faults, the body is very precious because of intelligence,

Left, A family of pilgrims walking into the main prayer hall of Sertang Monastery, Tagtsang Lhamo, Amdo, Eastern Tibet.

which we can use for many great works. Thus, when one's desire or attachment to one's body becomes extreme, it is very effective to meditate on the impure aspects of the body, particularly to reflect on its source, its constitution and its functions, so that one will have a more realistic and moderate outlook on the body.

Similarly, when our attitude toward our material possessions and wealth is not proper, it can lead to an extreme attachment toward such things as our property, houses, and belongings. This can lead to an inability to feel contented. If that happens, then one will always remain in a state of dissatisfaction, always wanting more. In a way, one is then really poor, because the suffering of poverty is the suffering of wanting something and feeling the lack of it. So even though one may have a lot of material possessions, if one is mentally poor, then one will always feel lacking and will always want more.

On the other hand, material facilities are quite crucial for society, because when individuals acquire material possessions and develop materially, it contributes in a way to the well-being of the society and the community. For that you need a certain degree of what I would call healthy competition, because without competition perhaps there might not be such good progress and material development. But it is still quite important to be aware of what type of competition we need, which is a sort of friendly competition that would not seek the destruction or the downfall of rivals or other people, but rather would act as a stimulating factor for growth and progress.

Personally, I can see some parallels between the need for competition in material development and spiritual development in Buddhism. In Buddhism, the foundation of the path is taking refuge in the Three Jewels: the Buddha, the

Right, A view of Dhankar Monastery in the late afternoon, dramatically perched on a ridge in the Spiti valley, India.

Dharma and the sangha (the spiritual community). The Buddha, being a fully Enlightened being, is very difficult to emulate. You may draw inspiration from the example of the Buddha, but you can't really compete with him, whereas when you take refuge in the sangha, the spiritual community, within the community there may be spiritual companions who are at the very beginning of the path to Enlightenment. When you reflect upon the qualities of the sangha, then you can get a sense of encouragement – you feel as if you can compete with the others. This is not really a negative competition; it is a healthy competition. Also, you can emulate the example of others ahead of you, with the confidence that you can reach their stage.

Now when we talk about objects of enjoyment or desire and material well-being, Buddhist literature mentions five types of object of desire: form, sound, odors, tastes, and tactile sensations.

Above, Monks with a ceremonial parasol going to prayers at Tashikhyil Monastery.
Left, A young monk practicing a sacred dance at Tashikhyil Monastery, Amdo, Eastern Tibet.

Whether or not these objects of enjoyment give rise to happiness, satisfaction, and contentment, or, conversely, give rise to suffering and dissatisfaction depends very much on how you apply your faculty of intelligence.

Similarly, just as in the case of material objects, one's relations to one's friends and companions have different potentials. In some cases, a certain type of interaction with one's friends or companions could lead to additional suffering, frustration, and dissatisfaction. A certain type of interaction can also lead to satisfaction, a sense of fulfillment, and happiness. Again, the outcome of our interactions depends upon the application of intelligence.

Another important issue is sexual relations. Sexual relations are part of nature and without them there would be no more human beings – that is clear. But to go to the extreme, to a sort of

Right, Fires of juniper incense
burning on hilltops at dawn beside
Nechung Monastery, Tibet.

> "Swans base their relationships solely on a sense of responsibility and they mate for life. This is very beautiful."

blind love, often creates problems and more misery. I think the main purpose of sexual relations is reproduction, the creation of beautiful new young babies. One must not have just the desire for sexual pleasure, but also a sense of responsibility, a sense of commitment. If we look at other species, I think some are very admirable. For example, certain birds, such as swans, base their relationships solely on a sense of responsibility and they mate for life. This is very beautiful! Some other animals, like dogs, do not have that kind of responsibility and just enjoy the sexual act, leaving the mother with the entire responsibility. This, I think, is awful!

I think as human beings we must follow nature, but the more civilized manner for sexual relations is not just to seek temporary satisfaction. If one does not see the sense of responsibility and

marriage, this is short-sighted. Sometimes people ask me about marriage. Of course I have no experience of it, but I am quite sure about one thing: marriage with too much haste is dangerous. First you must have a long period to examine one another and afterwards, when you have genuine confidence that you can live together, then you should marry. That is the proper way.

It seems that many families in these modern times have problems. One reason is that sexual freedom is too extreme. Moreover, part of your modern culture promotes sex and sexual things and I think this is not very healthy. On the other hand, if we compare sex with violence, then I think sex is better! But often because of sex, violence is also created. I think in reality they are very interlinked.

Right, Pilgrim and monks turning prayer wheels at Tashikhyil Monastery, Amdo, Eastern Tibet with a large chorten (reliquary) in the background.

While the most important thing in family life is children, birth control is also extremely important. Of course, from the Buddhist viewpoint, each individual human life is very precious. From that viewpoint, birth control is not good. But at the same time, the world's population is simply getting too great. Perhaps five billion people can be sustained if all the natural resources are utilized properly, and, according to some scientists, another two or three billion more may be acceptable. But I think it is better if we have a smaller number of people; this is more peaceful and more friendly. With this larger interest then, the conclusion is quite clear that we have to use birth control for the benefit of all humanity. Birth control is very necessary.

So, to repeat, our behavior in our daily lives is the key factor in determining whether all these facilities and relations really produce genuine, long-lasting satisfaction or not. Much depends on our own attitude. And for this mental factor, motivation is the key thing.

In Buddhist literature, human life is seen as a favorable form of existence or rebirth. There are various factors that could complement the favorable existence as a human being, such as having a long life, good health, material possessions, and eloquence so that one can relate to others in a more beneficial way. But as I pointed out earlier, whether or not these conditions can lead to a more beneficial existence or to a more harmful one depends very much on how you utilize them and whether or not you apply the faculty of intelligence.

On that point, Buddhist literature mentions the practice of the Six Perfections. For instance, in the case of acquiring material possessions, according to Buddhism, generosity and the act of giving are seen as causes of wealth. But in order to practice generosity and giving successfully, one

Left, A row of standing ritual bells and scepters (vajras) on an altar, which symbolize the union of wisdom (bell) and method (vajra).

"Good conduct is the way in which life becomes more meaningful, more constructive, and more peaceful."

must first of all have a sound ethical discipline, a certain type of outlook, and principles. And that ethical discipline or those principles can come about only if one has the ability to bear hardships and adverse circumstances when confronted with them. For that, you also need a certain degree of exertion or joyful effort. In order to practice the application of joyful effort successfully, one must have the ability to concentrate, to focus on events, actions, or goals. That in turn depends on whether or not you have the ability to exercise your power of judgment, to judge between what is desirable and what is undesirable, what is negative and what is positive. So, in a way, all these Six Perfections are related to the acquisition of even one of the conditions, say, material wealth.

How do we go about implementing in our daily lives the principles which are stipulated in the practice of the Six Perfections? Buddhism recommends living one's life within the ethical discipline of observance of what are known as the Ten Precepts, or Avoidance of the Ten Negative Actions. Out of these Ten Negative Actions, one, known as "wrong views" or "perverted views," might make more sense within the context of a religious belief. Other than that, all the other nine Negative Actions are, I would say, common denominators of all religious traditions. They are seen as negative or undesirable for society in general, regardless of any religious point of view.

To conclude, good conduct is the way in which life becomes more meaningful, more constructive, and more peaceful. For this, much depends on our own behavior and our own mental attitude.

Left, Monks walk past a colorful banner beside a building in Tashikhyil Monastery, Amdo, Eastern Tibet.

Facing Death
and Dying Well

Left, A large chorten (reliquary) at dusk above Ganden Monastery, Tibet.

The issue of facing death in a peaceful manner is a very difficult one. According to common sense, there seems to be two ways of dealing with the problem and the suffering. The first is simply to try to avoid the problem, to put it out of your mind, even though the reality of that problem is still there and it is not minimized. Another way of dealing with this issue is to look directly at the problem and analyze it, make it familiar to you and make it clear that it is a part of all our lives.

I have already touched on the topic of the body and illness. Illness happens. It is not something exceptional; it is part of nature and a fact of life. It happens because the body is there. Of course we have every right to avoid illness and pain, but in spite of that effort, when illness happens it is better to accept it. While you should make every effort to cure it as soon as possible, you should have no extra mental burden. As the great Indian scholar Shantideva has said: "If there is a way to overcome the suffering, then there is no need to worry; if there is no way to overcome the suffering, then there is no use in worrying." That kind of rational attitude is quite useful.

Now I want to speak about death. Death is a part of all our lives. Whether we like it or not, it is bound to happen. Instead of avoiding thinking about it, it is better to understand its meaning. On the news we often see murders and death, but some people seem to think that death happens only to others, not to themselves. That kind of attitude is wrong. We all have the same body, the same human flesh, and therefore we will all die. There is a big difference, of course, between natural death and accidental death, but basically death will come sooner or later. If from the beginning your attitude is, "Yes, death is part of our

Left, A painting of the Tibetan Wheel of Life on the wall of the Norbulingka Institute, Dharamsala, India.

"The success of our lives and our futures depends on our individual motivation and determination."

lives," then it may be easier to face. So there are two distinct approaches to dealing with a problem. One is to simply avoid it by not thinking about it. The other, which is much more effective, is to face it directly so that you are already conscious of it. Generally, there are two types of problem or suffering: with one type, it is possible that, by adopting a certain attitude, one will be able to actually reduce the force and level of suffering and anxiety. However, there could be other types of problem and suffering for which adopting a certain type of attitude and way of thinking may not necessarily reduce the level of suffering, but which would still prepare you to face it.

When unfortunate things happen in our lives there are two possible results. One possibility is mental unrest, anxiety, fear, doubt, frustration, and eventually depression, and, in the worst case, even suicide. That's one way. The other possibility is that because of that tragic experience you become more realistic,

you become closer to reality. With the power of investigation, the tragic experience may make you stronger and increase your self-confidence and self-reliance. The unfortunate event can be a source of inner strength.

The success of our lives and our futures, as I have said, depends on our individual motivation and determination or self-confidence. Through difficult experiences, life sometimes becomes more meaningful. If you look at people who, from the beginning of their lives, have had everything, you may see that when small things happen they soon lose hope or grow irritated. Others, like the generation of people in England who experienced World War II, have developed stronger mental attitudes as a result of their hardships. I think the person who has had more experience of hardships can stand more firmly in the face of problems than the person who has never experienced suffering. From this angle then, some suffering can be a good lesson for life.

Above, A pilgrim with a horse at a ceremony at Tashikhyil Monastery, Amdo, Eastern Tibet.

Now is this attitude just a way of deceiving oneself? Personally, I have lost my country and, worse still, in my country there has been a lot of destruction, suffering, and unhappiness. I have spent not only the majority of my life but also the best part of my life outside Tibet. If you think of this from that angle alone, there is hardly anything that is positive. But from another angle, you can see that because of these unfortunate things I have had another type of freedom, such as the opportunity of meeting different people from different traditions, and also of meeting scientists from different fields. From those experiences my life has been enriched and I have learned many valuable things. So my tragic experiences have also had some valuable aspects.

Looking at problems from these different angles actually lessens the mental burden or mental frustration. From the Buddhist viewpoint, every event has many aspects, and naturally, one event can be viewed from many, many different angles. It is very rare or almost impossible that an event can be negative from all points of view. Therefore, it is useful when something happens to try to look at it from different angles

Above, Young monks on the balcony of Tashikhyil Monastery.
Left, Designs in chalk on the ground in front of Tashikhyil, Amdo, Eastern Tibet.

Above, Woman beside new prayer flags just outside Lhasa, Tibet.

"Within the seed of the cause
of events is the seed for their
cessation and disintegration."

and then you can see the positive or beneficial aspects. Moreover, if something happens, it is very useful immediately to make a comparison with some other event or with the events of other people or other nations. This is also very helpful in sustaining your peace of mind.

I will now explain, as a Buddhist monk, how to deal with death. Buddha taught the principles of the Four Noble Truths, the first of which is the Truth of Suffering. The Truth of Suffering is taught within the context of three characteristics of existence, the first being impermanence. When talking about the nature of impermanence we must bear in mind that there are two levels. One is the coarse level, which is quite obvious and is the cessation of the continuation of a life or an event. But the impermanent nature which is being taught in relation to the Four Noble Truths refers to the more subtle aspect of impermanence, which is the transitory nature of existence.

Buddha's teaching of the more subtle aspects of the impermanent nature of existence aims at establishing an appreciation of the basic unsatisfactory nature of our existence. If you understand the nature of impermanence correctly, you will understand that it reveals that any existents which are causally produced, that is, which come about as a result of causes and conditions, entirely depend on causes and conditions for their existence.

Not only that, but the very causes and conditions which have produced them also bring about the disintegration and cessation of those very entities. So, within the seed of the cause of events is the seed for their cessation and disintegration. When this is related to the understanding of the impermanent nature of our own aggregates, the body and mind, then here the cause refers to our own ignorant state of mind, which is the root of our existence, and this reveals that our very physical existence, our bodily existence, is very much governed by the force of an ignorant state of mind.

But it is by first reflecting upon the coarser levels of impermanence that one is eventually led to an appreciation of the subtle levels of impermanence. And by this, one will be able to confront and counteract grasping at permanence or eternal existence of one's own identity or self, because it is this grasping at permanence that forces us to cling onto this very "now-ness" or matters of one's lifetime alone. By releasing the grip of this grasping and enduring within us, we will be in a better position to appreciate the value of working for our future lifetimes.

One of the reasons why awareness of death and impermanence is so crucial in the Buddhist religious practice is that it is considered that your state of mind at the time of death has a very great effect on determining what form of rebirth you might take. Whether it is a positive

*Left, Pilgrims and a monk turning prayer wheels
while performing a "kora" or circumambulation
of Tashikhyil Monastery, Amdo, Eastern Tibet.*

"Buddhist practice greatly emphasizes the importance of the awareness of death and impermanence."

state of mind or a negative one will have a great effect. Therefore, Buddhist religious practice greatly emphasizes the importance of the awareness of death and impermanence.

Although the main purpose of a high degree of awareness of impermanence is to train oneself so that at the time of death one will be in a virtuous and positive state of mind, and will be assured of a positive rebirth, there are other benefits. One of the positive side-effects of maintaining a very high degree of awareness of death is that it will prepare the individual to such an extent that, when the individual actually faces death, he or she will be in a better position to maintain his or her presence of mind. Especially in Tantric Buddhism, it is considered that the state of mind which one experiences at the point of death is extremely subtle

and, because of the subtlety of the level of that consciousness, it also has a great power and impact upon one's mental continuum. So in Tantric practices we find a lot of emphasis placed on death-related meditations and also reflections upon the process of death, so that the individual at the time of death not only retains his or her presence of mind, but also is in a position to utilize that subtle state of consciousness effectively toward the realization of the path.

It is because of this that we find many Tantric meditations, technically known as the "deity yoga meditations" because they are meditations on deities, involve the dissolution process, reflecting upon the dissolution of elements which the individual experiences at the point of death. In fact, from the Tantric

Right, His Holiness the Dalai Lama teaching at the Kalachakra Initiation, Spiti, India, August, 2000.

perspective, the entire process of existence is explained in terms of the three stages known as "death," "the intermediate state," and "rebirth." All of these three stages of existence are seen as states or manifestations of the consciousness and the energies that accompany or propel the consciousness, so that the intermediate state and rebirth are nothing other than various levels of the subtle consciousness and energy. An example of such fluctuating states can be found in our daily existence, when during the 24-hour day we go through a cycle of deep sleep, the waking period and the dream state. Our daily existence is in fact characterized by these three stages.

When talking about the distinctions that are made in the Tantric literature between the subtle and gross levels of consciousness and mind, I think it is important to bear in mind what exactly we mean by "mental consciousness."

Often people get the impression that when we talk about the sixth mental consciousness there is some kind of autonomous type of consciousness which is totally independent from the bodily states and which is, in a way, the equivalent of the soul. But this is a misunderstanding. I personally think that if we were to examine our mental world we would find that most of our mental states and mental functions have direct physical correlates. Not only the sensory consciousness, but also much of what we would call mental consciousness has physiological bases and is intimately linked with the bodily states, just as scientists would say that the brain and nervous system are the primary physiological bases of much of our conscious experience. Therefore, when the bodily states cease, these mental functions also cease.

But the question really is: what makes it possible for certain physical substances or

Left, Monks attend an altar beneath a large thangka of Vaishravana, the yellow God of wealth and guardian king of the northern quarter, Tashikhyil Monastery, Amdo, Eastern Tibet.

physiological states to give rise to a mental event or a state of awareness? The Buddhist, particularly the Tantric, explanation points toward what is known as the subtle Clear Light state, which can be seen as independent from a physiological base. And it is this Clear Light state of mind which is the most subtle level of consciousness which, when it interacts with the physiological base, gives rise to all our conscious and cognitive events.

There are certain indications of the existence of what we call the Clear Light state of mind. There are incidents which generally tend to be more possible for religious practitioners. For instance, among the Tibetan community in exile there have been cases where people have been pronounced clinically dead, that is, their brain function has ceased and the brain is dead but the decomposition of the body has not begun, and they remain in that state for days on end. For instance, my own late tutor, Kyabje Ling Rinpoche, remained in that state for 13 days. He was pronounced clinically dead and he had already experienced the death of the brain, but his body remained fresh and did not decompose for 13 days.

Now there must be some explanation for this. The Buddhist explanation is that, during that state, the individual is not actually dead but rather in the process of dying. Buddhists would explain that although the mind–body relationship may have ceased at the grosser, coarse level, it has not ceased at the subtle level. According to particular Tantric literature known as the Guhyasamaja Tantra, when an individual goes through the process of death, there is a certain process of dissolution. From that dissolution into the Clear Light state there is a reversal cycle and when that cycle reaches a certain stage, a new life begins that is called

Right, A young monk leading an old monk on horseback near Phuhktal Monastery, Zanskar, India.

the rebirth. Then that rebirth remains and the individual again goes through a process of dissolution. In a way, death is at the intervening stage when the elements dissolve into the Clear Light and from there re-arise in another form. So death is nothing other than these intervening points when the individual's various physiological elements dissolve into the Clear Light point.

As regards the actual dissolution process of the various elements, the literature mentions different stages of dissolution and their accom-panying signs. For instance, in the case of the dissolution of the coarser levels of elements, there are both internal and external signs and indications that mark the dissolution. When it comes to the subtle elements, there are only internal signs such as visions and so forth. There has been a growing interest among scientists who are doing research on death in these descriptions of the dissolution processes, particularly the internal and external signs. As a Buddhist, I think it is very important for us to be aware of the scientific investigations that are

Above, A monk making a ritual hand gesture (mudra) with his prayer beads, representing the ultimate offering of the universe as a mandala, Dharamsala, India. Right, A monk at Tabo Monastery, Spiti, India.

being undertaken. However, we must be able to distinguish between phenomena which still remain beyond the verification of existing scientific methodology and phenomena which can be seen as being disproved by existing scientific methods and investigation. I would say that if certain phenomena can be seen as being disproved by science, through scientific investigation and scientific methods, I think as Buddhists we will have to respect those conclusions.

As death becomes something familiar to you, as you have some knowledge of its processes and can recognize its external and internal indications, you are prepared for it. According to my own experience, I still have no confidence that at the moment of death I will really implement all these practices for which I have prepared. I have no guarantee!

*Left, A sacred masked dance
at the Monlam Prayer Festival,
Tashikhyil Monastery,
Amdo, Eastern Tibet.*

"Sometimes when I think about death I have a feeling of curiosity and this makes it much easier for me to accept death."

However, sometimes when I think about death I get some kind of excitement. Instead of fear, I have a feeling of curiosity and this makes it much easier for me to accept death. I wonder to what extent I can implement these practices. Of course, my only burden if I die today is, "Oh, what will happen to Tibet? What about Tibetan culture? What about the six million Tibetan people's rights?" This is my main concern. Otherwise, I feel almost no fear of death. Perhaps I have some kind of blind confidence! So it is good to reduce the fear of death. In my daily practice of prayer I visualize eight different deity yogas and eight different deaths. Perhaps when death comes all my preparation may fail. I hope not!

Anyway, I think that way is mentally very helpful in dealing with death. Even if there is no next life, there is some benefit if it relieves fear. And because there is less fear, one can be more fully prepared. Just as for battle, without preparation there is a good chance you will lose, but if you are fully prepared, there is more chance of defense. If you are fully prepared then, at the moment of death, you can retain your peace of mind. It is peace of mind at the time of death which is the foundation for cultivating the proper motivation and that is the immediate guarantee of a good rebirth, of a better life to come. Particularly for the practitioner of the Maha-anuttarayoga Tantrayana, death is one of the rare opportunities to transform the subtle mind into wisdom.

As to what is in store for us after death, Buddhists talk about three realms of existence, technically known as "the form realm," "the

Right, A young monk beside a door of the main prayer hall of Tashikhyil Monastery, Amdo, Eastern Tibet.

formless realm," and "the desire realm." Both the form realm and the desire realm have an intervening stage before you take rebirth, known as "the intermediate state." What all of this points toward is that although the occasion of death provides us with the best opportunity to utilize our most subtle level of consciousness, transforming it into a path of wisdom, even if we are not able to seize that opportunity effectively, there is an intermediate state which, though grosser than at the time of death, is a lot more subtle than the consciousness at the time of rebirth. So there is another opportunity. And even if we are unable to seize this opportunity, there is rebirth and a continuing cycle.

So in order to seize the wonderful opportunity accorded at the time of death and, after that, during the intermediate state, we need first to train ourselves to be able to utilize those moments. For that, Buddhism teaches various techniques to enable the individual to apply certain meditative techniques during each of the dream, deep sleep, and waking states.

In conclusion, I think at the time of death a peaceful mind is essential no matter what you believe in, whether it is Buddhism or some other religion. At the moment of death, the individual should not seek to develop anger, hatred, and so on. That is very important at the conventional level. I think even non-believers see that it is better to pass away in a peaceful manner. It is much happier. Also, for those who believe in heaven or some other concept, it is also best to pass away peacefully with the thought of one's own God or belief in higher forces. For Buddhists and also other ancient Indian traditions which accept the rebirth or karma theory, naturally at the time of death a virtuous state of mind is beneficial.

Left, Young monks exchanging conversation during a ceremony at Tashikhyil Monastery, Amdo, Eastern Tibet.

Dealing with Anger and Emotion

"According to my experience, it is clear that if each individual makes an effort then he or she can change."

Anger and hatred are two of our closest friends. When I was young I had quite a close relationship with anger. Then eventually I found a lot of disagreement with anger. By using common sense, with the help of compassion and wisdom, I now have a more powerful argument with which to defeat anger.

According to my experience, it is clear that if each individual makes an effort then he or she can change. Of course, change is not immediate and it takes a lot of time. In order to change and deal with emotions it is crucial to analyze which thoughts are useful, constructive, and of benefit to us. I mean mainly those thoughts which make us calmer, more relaxed, and which give us peace of mind, versus those thoughts which create uneasiness, fear, and frustration. This analysis is similar to one which we might use for external things, such as plants. Some plants, flowers, and fruit are good for us, so we use them and grow them. Those plants which are poisonous or harmful to us, we learn to recognize and even sometimes to destroy.

There is a similarity with the inner world. It is too simplistic to speak about the "body" and the "mind." Within the body there are billions of different particles. Similarly, there are many different thoughts and a variety of states of mind. It is wise to take a close look into the world of your mind and to make the distinction between beneficial and harmful states of mind. Once you can recognize the value of good states of mind, you can increase or foster them.

Buddha taught the principles of the Four Noble Truths and these form the foundation of

Left, A detailed close-up of the hands of a pilgrim woman wearing a fine chuba at Tashikhyil Monastery, Amdo, Eastern Tibet.

the Buddha Dharma. The Third Noble Truth is cessation. According to Nagarjuna, in this context cessation means the state of mind or mental quality which, through practice and effort, ceases all the negative emotions. Nagarjuna defines true cessation as a state in which the individual has reached a perfected state of mind which is free from the effects of various afflictive and negative emotions and thoughts. Such a state of true cessation is, according to Buddhism, a genuine Dharma and therefore is the refuge that all practising Buddhists seek. Buddha becomes an object of refuge, worthy of respect, because Buddha has realized that state. Therefore one's reverence to the Buddha, and the reason one seeks refuge in the Buddha, is not because Buddha was from the beginning a special person, but because Buddha realized the state of true cessation. Similarly, the spiritual community, or sangha, is taken as an object of refuge because the members of the spiritual community are individuals who are either already on, or are embarking on, the path leading to that state of cessation.

We find that the true state of cessation can be understood only in terms of a state of mind which is free from, or which has been purified of, negative emotions and thoughts due to the application of antidotes and counter-forces. True cessation is a state of mind and the factors that lead to this are also functions of the mind. Also, the basis on which the purification takes place is the mental continuum. Therefore, an understanding of the nature of the mind is crucial for Buddhist practice. By saying this, I do not mean that everything which exists is simply a reflection or projection of the mind and that apart from the mind nothing exists. But because of the importance

Right, Monks in full ceremonial attire walking to an early morning prayer ceremony, Tashikhyil Monastery.

of understanding the nature of mind in Buddhist practice, people often describe Buddhism as "a science of the mind."

Generally speaking, in Buddhist literature, a negative emotion or thought is defined as "a state which causes disturbance within one's mind." These afflictive emotions and thoughts are factors that create unhappiness and turmoil within us. Emotion in general is not necessarily something negative. At a scientific conference which I attended along with many psychologists and neuro-scientists, it was concluded that even Buddhas have emotion, according to the definition of emotion found in various scientific disciplines. So karuna (infinite compassion or kindness) can be described as a kind of emotion.

Naturally, emotions can be positive and negative. However, when talking about anger, etc., we are dealing with negative emotions.

Above, Spinning prayer wheels, Tashikhyil Monastery, Amdo, Eastern Tibet.
Left, The entrance to the main prayer hall of Sertang Monastery, Tagtsang Lhamo, Amdo, Eastern Tibet.

Above, A young monk in ceremonial costume participating in a sacred dance,
Tashikhyil Monastery, Amdo, Eastern Tibet.

"There are meditative techniques which enable the transformation of the energy of anger."

Negative emotions are those which immediately create some kind of unhappiness or uneasiness and which, in the long run, create certain actions. Those actions ultimately lead to harm to others, and this brings pain or suffering to oneself. This is what we mean by negative emotions.

One negative emotion is anger. Perhaps there are two types of anger. One type of anger could be transformed into a positive emotion. For example, if one has a sincere compassionate motivation and concern for someone, and that person does not heed one's warning about his or her actions, then there is no other alternative except the use of some kind of force to stop that person's misdeeds. In Tantrayana practice there are meditative techniques which enable the transformation of the energy of anger. This is the reason behind the wrathful deities. On the basis of compassionate motivation, anger may in some cases be useful because it gives us extra energy and enables us to act swiftly.

However, anger usually leads to hatred and hatred is always negative. Hatred harbours ill will. I usually analyze anger on two levels: on the basic human level and on the Buddhist level. From the human level, without any reference to a religious tradition or ideology, we can look at the sources of our happiness: good health, material facilities, and good companions. Now from the standpoint of health, negative emotions such as hatred are very bad. Since people generally try to take care of their health, one technique people can use is their mental attitude. Your mental state should always remain calm. Even if some anxiety occurs, as it is bound to in life, you should always be calm. Like a wave which rises from the water and dissolves back into the water, these disturbances are very short, so they should not affect your basic mental attitude. Though you cannot eliminate all negative emotions, if your basic mental attitude is healthy and calm, it will not be much affected. If

you remain calm, your blood pressure and so on remains more normal and as a result your health will improve. While I cannot say scientifically why this is so, I believe that my own physical condition is improving as I get older. I have had the same medicine, the same doctor, the same food, so it must be due to my mental state. Some people say to me, "You must have some kind of special Tibetan medicine." But I don't!

As I mentioned earlier, when I was young I was quite short-tempered. I would sometimes excuse this by saying that it was because my father was short-tempered, as if it was something genetic. But as time passes, I think that now I have almost no hatred toward anybody, including toward those Chinese who are creating misery and suffering for Tibetans. Even toward them, I really do not feel any kind of hatred.

Right, A chorten (reliquary) in a field
after a fresh snow fall, near Lhasa, Tibet.

Some of my close friends have high blood pressure, yet they never come near to having crises in their health and they never feel tired. Over the years I have met some very good practitioners. Meanwhile, there are other friends who have great material comfort yet, when we start to talk, after the initial few nice words, they begin to complain and grieve. In spite of their material prosperity, these people do not have calm or peaceful minds. As a result, they are always worrying about their digestion, their sleep, everything! Therefore it is clear that mental calmness is a very important factor for good health. If you want good health, don't ask a doctor, look within yourself. Try to utilize some of your potential. This even costs less!

The second source of happiness is material facilities. Sometimes when I wake up in the early morning, if my mood is not very good, then when I look at my watch I feel uncomfortable because of my mood. Then on other days, due perhaps to the previous day's experience, when I wake up my mood is pleasant and peaceful. At that time, when I look at my watch I see it as extraordinarily beautiful. Yet it is the same watch, isn't it? The difference comes from my mental attitude. Whether our use of our material facilities provides genuine satisfaction or not depends on our mental attitude.

It is bad for our material facilities if our mind is dominated by anger. To speak again from my own experience, when I was young I sometimes repaired watches. I tried and failed many times. Sometimes I would lose my patience and hit the watch! During those moments, my anger altered my whole attitude and afterwards I felt very sorry for my actions. If my goal was to repair the watch, then why did I hit it on the table? Again you can see how one's mental attitude is crucial in order to

Right, Pilgrims performing a "kora" or circumambulation of a large chorten (reliquary), Tashikhyil Monastery, Amdo, Eastern Tibet.

"It is obvious that when you are mentally calm you are honest and open-minded."

utilize material facilities for one's genuine satisfaction or benefit.

The third source of happiness is our companions. It is obvious that when you are mentally calm you are honest and open-minded. I will give you an example. Perhaps 14 or 15 years ago, there was an Englishman named Phillips who had a close relationship with the Chinese government, including Chou En Lai and other leaders. He had known them for many years and he was close friends with the Chinese. One time, in 1977 or 1978, Phillips came to Dharamsala to see me. He brought some films with him and he told me about all the good aspects of China. At the beginning of our meeting there was a big disagreement between us, for we held completely different opinions. In his view, the presence of the Chinese in Tibet was something good. In my opinion, and according to many reports, the situation was not good. As usual, I had no particular negative feeling toward him. I just felt that he held these views due to ignorance. With openness, I continued our conversation. I argued that those Tibetans who had joined the Chinese Communist Party as early as 1930 and who had participated in the Sino–Japanese War and had welcomed the Chinese invasion and enthusiastically collaborated with the Chinese Communists did so because they believed that it was a golden opportunity to develop Tibet, from the viewpoint of Marxist ideology. These people had collaborated with the Chinese out of genuine hope. Then, around 1956 or 1957, most of them were dismissed from the various Chinese offices, some were

Left, A monk playing a short ritual horn in a ceremony at the Jokhang Temple, Lhasa, Tibet. This instrument is modelled upon the form of a human thighbone trumpet.

Above, A monk walking down a snowy path towards Tashikhyil Monastery, Amdo, Eastern Tibet.
Right, A detail of a monk's robe and ceremonial hat, Tashikhyil Monastery.

imprisoned, and others disappeared. Thus I explained that we are not anti-Chinese or anti-Communist. In fact, I sometimes think of myself as a half-Marxist, half-Buddhist. I explained all these different things to him with sincere motivation and openness and after some time his attitude completely changed. This instance gives me some confirmation that even if there is a big difference of opinion, you can communicate on a human level. You can put aside these different opinions and communicate as human beings. I think that is one way to create positive feelings in other people's minds.

Also, I am quite sure that if this Fourteenth Dalai Lama smiled less, perhaps I would have fewer friends in various places. My attitude toward other people is to always look at them from the human level. On that level, whether president, queen or beggar, there is no difference, provided that there is genuine human feeling with a genuine human smile of affection.

I think that there is more value in genuine human feeling than in status and so on. I am just a simple human being. Through my experience and mental discipline, a certain new attitude has developed. This is nothing special. You, who I think have had a better education and more experience than myself, have more potential to change within yourself. I come from a small village with no modern education and no deep awareness of the world. Also,

from the age of 15 or 16 I had an unthinkable sort of burden. Therefore each of you should feel that you have great potential and that, with self-confidence and a little more effort, change really is possible if you want it. If you feel that your present way of life is unpleasant or has some difficulties, then don't look at these negative things. See the positive side, the potential, and make an effort. I think that there is already at that point some kind of partial guarantee of success. If we utilize all our positive human energy or human qualities we can overcome these human problems.

So, as far as our contact with fellow human beings is concerned, our mental attitude is very crucial. Even for a non-believer, just a simple honest human being, the ultimate source of happiness is in our mental attitude. Even if you have good health, material facilities used in the proper way, and good relations with other human beings, the main cause of a happy life is within. If you have more money you sometimes have more worries and you still feel hungry for more. Ultimately you become a slave of money. While money is very useful and necessary, it is not the ultimate source of happiness. Similarly, education, if not well balanced, can sometimes create more trouble, more anxiety, more greed, more desire, and more ambition – in short, more mental suffering. Friends, too, are sometimes very troublesome.

Now you can see how to minimize anger and hatred. First, it is extremely important to realize the negativity of these emotions in general, particularly hatred. I consider hatred to be the ultimate enemy. By "enemy" I mean the person or factor which directly or indirectly destroys our interest. Our interest is that which ultimately creates happiness.

We can also speak of the external enemy. For example, in my own case, our Chinese brothers and sisters are destroying Tibetan

Right, The ornately decorated doors of a prayer hall in Tashikhyil Monastery, Amdo, Eastern Tibet.

Above, Monks seated in meditation on the steps of Tashikhyil Monastery, Amdo, Eastern Tibet.

"Once you try to control or discipline your anger, then eventually even big events will not cause anger."

rights and, in that way, more suffering and anxiety develop. But no matter how forceful this is, it cannot destroy the supreme source of my happiness, which is my calmness of mind. This is something an external enemy cannot destroy. Our country can be invaded, our possessions can be destroyed, our friends can be killed, but these are secondary for our mental happiness. The ultimate source of my mental happiness is my peace of mind. Nothing can destroy this except my own anger.

Moreover, you can escape or hide from an external enemy and sometimes you can even cheat the enemy. For example, if there is someone who disturbs my peace of mind, I can escape by locking my door and sitting quietly alone. But I cannot do that with anger! Wherever I go, it is always there. Even though I have locked my room, the anger is still inside. Unless you adopt a certain method, there is no possibility of escape. Therefore, hatred or anger – and here I mean negative anger – is

ultimately the real destroyer of my peace of mind and is therefore my true enemy.

Some people believe that to suppress emotion is not good, that it is much better to let it out. I think there are differences between various negative emotions. For example, with frustration, there is a certain frustration which develops as a result of past events. Sometimes if you hide these negative events, such as sexual abuse, then consciously or unconsciously this creates problems. Therefore, in this case, it is much better to express the frustration and let it out. However, according to our experience with anger, if you do not make an attempt to reduce it, it will remain with you and even increase. Then even with small incidents you will immediately get angry. Once you try to control or discipline your anger, then eventually even big events will not cause anger. Through training and discipline you can change.

When anger comes, there is one important technique to help you keep your peace of

mind. You should not become dissatisfied or frustrated, because this is the cause of anger and hatred. There is a natural connection between cause and effect. Once certain causes and conditions are fully met, it is extremely difficult to prevent that causal process from coming to fruition. It is crucial to examine the situation so that at a very early stage one is able to put a stop to the causal process. Then it does not continue to an advanced stage. In the Buddhist text *Guide to the Bodhisattva Way of Life*, the great scholar Shantideva mentions that it is very important to ensure that a person does not get into a situation which leads to dissatisfaction, because dissatisfaction is the seed of anger. This means that one must adopt a certain outlook toward one's material possessions, toward one's

Left, The Potala Palace,
the traditional historical abode
of His Holiness the Dalai Lama
at dawn in Lhasa, Tibet.

"By bringing about a change in our outlook toward things and events, all phenomena can become sources of happiness."

companions and friends, and toward various situations.

Our feelings of dissatisfaction, unhappiness, loss of hope, and so forth are in fact related to all phenomena. If we do not adopt the right outlook, it is possible that anything and everything could cause us frustration. For some people even the name of the Buddha could conceivably cause anger and frustration, although it may not be the case when someone has a direct personal encounter with a Buddha. Therefore, all phenomena have the potential to create frustration and dissatisfaction in us. Yet phenomena are part of reality and we are subject to the laws of existence. So this leaves us only one option: to change our own attitude. By bringing about a change in our outlook toward things and events, all phenomena can become friends or sources of happiness, instead of becoming enemies or sources of frustration.

A particular case is that of an enemy. Of course, in one way, having an enemy is very bad. It disturbs our mental peace and destroys some of our good things. But if we look at it from another angle, only an enemy gives us the opportunity to practice patience. No one else provides us with the opportunity for tolerance. For example, as a Buddhist, I think Buddha completely failed to provide us with the opportunity to practice tolerance and patience. Some members of the sangha may provide us with this, but otherwise it is quite rare. Since we do not know the majority of the five billion human beings on this earth, therefore the majority of people do not give us an opportunity to show

Right, The "Emblem of the Three Great Bodhisattvas" with the sword
representing Manjushri's widsom, the parrot Vajrapani's power and the duck
Avalokiteshvara's compassion, Tashikhyil Monastery.

tolerance or patience either. Only those people whom we know and who create problems for us really provide us with a good opportunity to practice tolerance and patience.

Seen from this angle, the enemy is the greatest teacher for our practice. Shantideva argues very brilliantly that enemies, or the perpetrators of harm upon us, are in fact objects worthy of respect and are worthy of being regarded as our precious teachers. One might object that our enemies cannot be considered worthy of our respect because they have no intention of helping us; the fact that they are helpful and beneficial to us is merely a coincidence. Shantideva says that if this is the case then why should we, as practicing Buddhists, regard the state of cessation as an object worthy of refuge when cessation is a mere state of mind and on its part has no intention of helping us. One may then say that although this is true, at least with cessation there is no intention of harming us, whereas enemies, contrary to having the intention of helping us, in fact intend to harm us. Therefore an enemy is not an object worthy of respect. Shantideva says that it is this very intention of harming us which makes the enemy very special. If the enemy had no intention of harming us, then we would not classify that person as an enemy, therefore our attitude would be completely different. It is his or her very intention of harming us which makes that person an enemy, and because of that the enemy provides us with an opportunity to practice tolerance and patience. Therefore an enemy is indeed a precious teacher. By thinking along these lines you can eventually reduce the negative mental emotions, particularly hatred.

Sometimes people feel that anger is useful because it brings extra energy and boldness. When we encounter difficulties, we may see

Left, A monk wearing the brocade robes, bone ornaments and skull crown of a tantric deity while performing a sacred dance at Sertang Monastery.

"One can overcome the forces of negative emotions, like anger and hatred, by cultivating their counter-forces, like love and compassion."

anger as a protector. But though anger brings us more energy, that energy is essentially a blind one. There is no guarantee that that anger and energy will not become destructive to our own interests. Therefore hatred and anger are not at all useful.

Another question is that if you always remain humble then others may take advantage of you and how should you react? It is quite simple: you should act with wisdom or common sense, without anger and hatred. If the situation is such that you need some sort of action on your part, you can, without anger, take a counter-measure. In fact, such actions which follow true wisdom rather than anger are in reality more effective. A counter-measure taken in the midst of anger may often go wrong. In a very competitive society, it is sometimes necessary to take a counter-measure. We can again examine the Tibetan situation. As I mentioned earlier, we are following a genuinely non-violent and compassionate way, but this

does not mean that we should just bow down to the aggressors' action and give in. Without anger and without hatred, we can manage more effectively.

There is another type of practice of tolerance which involves consciously taking on the sufferings of others. I am thinking of situations in which, by engaging in certain activities, we are aware of the hardships, difficulties, and problems that are involved in the short term, but are convinced that such actions will have a very beneficial long-term effect. Because of our attitude, and our commitment and wish to bring about that long-term benefit, we sometimes consciously and deliberately take upon ourselves the hardships and problems that are involved in the short term.

One of the effective means by which one can overcome the forces of negative emotions like anger and hatred is by cultivating their counter-forces, such as the positive qualities of mind like love and compassion.

Above, "Mani" stones (stones with prayers and symbols inscribed on them) beside a chorten (reliquary) on the route to Phuktal Monastery in Zanskar, India.

Giving and Receiving

Left, A view out of a window of Dhankar Monastery, Spiti, India.

Compassion is the most wonderful and precious thing. When we talk about compassion, it is encouraging to note that basic human nature is, I believe, compassionate and gentle. Sometimes I argue with friends who believe that human nature is more negative and aggressive. I argue that if you study the structure of the human body you will see that it is akin to those species of mammals whose way of life is more gentle or peaceful. Sometimes I half joke that our hands are arranged in such a manner that they are good for hugging, rather than hitting. If our hands were mainly meant for hitting, then these beautiful fingers would not be necessary. For example, if the fingers remain extended, boxers cannot hit forcefully, so they have to make fists. So I think that means that our basic physical structure creates a compassionate or gentle kind of nature.

If we look at relationships, marriage and conception are very important. As I said earlier, marriage should not be based on blind love or an extreme sort of mad love; it should be based on a knowledge of one another and an understanding that you are suitable to live together. Marriage is not for temporary satisfaction, but for some kind of sense of responsibility. That is the genuine love which is the basis of marriage.

The proper conception of a child takes place in that kind of moral or mental attitude. While the child is in the mother's womb, the mother's calmness of mind has a very positive effect on the unborn child, according to some scientists. If the mother's mental state is negative, for instance if she is frustrated or angry, then it is very harmful to the healthy development of the unborn child. One scientist has told me that the first few weeks after birth is the most important period, for during that time the

Left, Chorten and prayer flags at dawn on the Kunzum La pass between the Spiti valley and Lahaul, Himachal Pradesh, India.

"Lessons we learn from teachers who are not just good, but who also show affection for the student, go deep into our minds."

child's brain is growing. During that period, the mother's touch or that of someone who is acting like a mother is crucial. This shows that even though the child may not realize who is who, it somehow physically needs someone else's affection. Without that, it is very damaging for the healthy development of the brain.

After birth, the first act by the mother is to give the child nourishing milk. If the mother lacks affection or kind feelings for the child, then the milk will not flow. If the mother feeds her baby with gentle feelings toward the child, in spite of her own illness or pain, as a result the milk flows freely. This kind of attitude is like a precious jewel. Moreover, from the other side, if the child lacks some kind of close feeling toward the mother, it may not suckle. This shows how wonderful the act of affection from both sides is. That is the beginning of our lives.

Similarly with education, it is my experience that those lessons which we learn from teachers who are not just good, but who also show affection for the student, go deep into our minds. Lessons from other sorts of teachers may not. Although you may be compelled to study and may fear the teacher, the lessons may not sink in. Much depends on the affection from the teacher.

Likewise, when we go to a hospital, irrespective of the doctor's quality, if the doctor shows genuine feeling and deep concern for us, and if he or she smiles, then we feel OK. But if the doctor shows little human affection, then even though he or she may be a very great expert, we may feel unsure and nervous. This is human nature.

Lastly, we can reflect on our lives. When we are young and again when we are old, we depend heavily on the affection of others. Between these stages we usually feel that we can do everything without help from others and that other people's affection is simply not important. But at this stage I think it is very important to keep deep human affection. When people in a

Above, The bronze head of a mythical sea monster (Makara) and a strutting dragon adorn the roof of a prayer hall at Tashikhyil Monastery.

big town or city feel lonely, this does not mean that they lack human companions, but rather that they lack human affection. As a result of this, their mental health eventually becomes very poor. On the other hand, those people who grow up in an atmosphere of human affection have a much more positive and gentle development of their bodies, their minds, and their behavior. Children who have grown up lacking that atmosphere usually have more negative attitudes. This very clearly shows the basic human nature. Also, as I have mentioned, the human body appreciates peace of mind. Things that are disturbing to us have a very bad effect upon our health. This shows that the whole structure of our health is such that it is suited to an atmosphere of human affection. Therefore, our potential for compassion is there. The only issue is whether or not we realize this and utilize it.

The basic aim of my explanation is to show that by nature we are compassionate, that compassion is something very necessary, and something which we can develop. It is important to know the exact meaning of compassion. Different philosophies and traditions have different interpretations of the meaning of love and compassion. Some of my Christian friends believe that love cannot develop without God's grace; in other words, to develop love and compassion you need faith. The Buddhist interpretation is that genuine compassion is based on a clear acceptance or recognition that others, like oneself, want happiness and have the right to overcome suffering. On that basis one develops some kind of concern about the welfare of others, irrespective of one's attitude to oneself. That is compassion.

Your love and compassion toward your friends is in many cases actually attachment. This feeling is not based on the realization that

Left, Monks and nuns and lay people at the Kalachakra Initiation ceremony at Ki Monastery, Spiti, India.

Above, Monks waiting for dawn to unfurl a giant thangkha at Sertang Monastery,
Tagtsang Lhamo, Amdo, Eastern Tibet on the 13th day of the Monlam prayer festival.

"All sentient beings should be looked on as equal. You can then gradually develop genuine compassion for all of them.

all beings have an equal right to be happy and to overcome suffering. Instead, it is based on the idea that something is "mine," "my friend," or something good for "me." That is attachment. Thus, when that person's attitude toward you changes, your feeling of closeness immediately disappears. With the other way, you develop some kind of concern irrespective of the other person's attitude to you, simply because that person is a fellow human being and has every right to overcome suffering. Whether that person remains neutral to you or even becomes your enemy, your concern should remain because of his or her right. That is the main difference. Genuine compassion is much healthier; it is unbiased, and it is based on reason. By contrast, attachment is narrow-minded and biased.

Actually, genuine compassion and attachment are contradictory. According to Buddhist practice, to develop genuine compassion you must first practice the meditation of equalization and equanimity, detaching oneself from those people who are very close to you. Then, you must remove negative feelings toward your enemies. All sentient beings should be looked on as equal. On that basis, you can gradually develop genuine compassion for all of them. It must be said that genuine compassion is not like pity or a feeling that others are somehow lower than yourself. Rather, with genuine compassion you view others as more important than yourself.

As I pointed out earlier, in order to generate genuine compassion, first of all one must go through the training of equanimity. This becomes very important, because without a sense of equanimity toward all, one's feelings toward others will be biased. So now I will give you a brief example of a Buddhist meditative training on developing equanimity. First, you should think about a small group of people whom you know, such as your friends and

relatives, toward whom you have attachment. Second, you should think about some people to whom you feel totally indifferent. And third, think about some people whom you dislike. Once you have imagined these different people, you should try to let your mind go into its natural state and see how it would normally respond to an encounter with these people. You will notice that your natural reaction would be that of attachment toward your friends, that of dislike toward the people whom you consider enemies, and that of total indifference toward those whom you consider neutral. Then you should try to question yourself. You should compare the effects of the two opposing attitudes you have toward your friends and your enemies, and see why you should have such fluctuating states of mind toward these two different groups of people.

*Right, Monks and pilgrims
gather around a giant thangkha in
a ceremony at Sertang Monastery.*

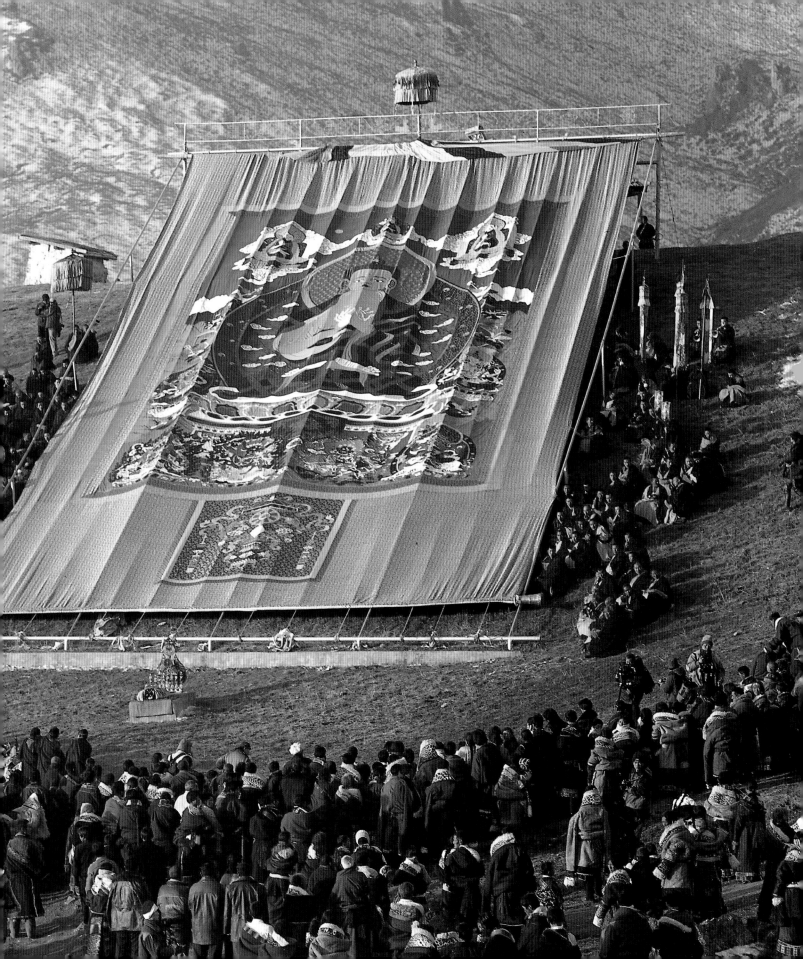

You should see what effects such reactions have on your mind and try to see the futility of relating to them in such an extreme manner. I have already discussed the pros and cons of harboring hatred and generating anger toward enemies, and I have also spoken a little about the defects of being extremely attached toward friends and so on. You should reflect upon this and then try to minimize your strong emotions toward these two opposing groups of people. Then, most importantly, you should reflect on the fundamental equality between yourself and all other sentient beings. Just as you have the instinctive natural desire to be happy and overcome suffering, so do all sentient beings; just as you have the right to fulfil this innate

Above, Monks holding a parasol, victory banners and ritual hand drums.
Left, Monks in front of a giant thangkha in a ceremony at Sertang Monastery.

"The only option is to live and work together harmoniously, and keep in our minds the interest of the whole of humanity."

aspiration, so do all sentient beings. So on what exact grounds do you discriminate?

If we look at humanity as a whole, we are social animals. Moreover, the structures of the modern economy, education, and so on, illustrate that the world has become a smaller place and that we depend heavily on one another. Under such circumstances, I think the only option is to live and work together harmoniously, and keep in our minds the interest of the whole of humanity. That is the only outlook and way we must adopt for our survival.

By nature, especially as a human being, my interests are not independent of others. My happiness depends on others' happiness. So when I see happy people, automatically I also feel a little bit happier than when I see people in a difficult situation. For example, when we see pictures on television which show people starving in Somalia, including old people and young children, then we automatically feel sad, regardless of whether that sadness can lead to some kind of active help or not.

Moreover, in our daily lives we are now utilizing many good facilities, including things like air-conditioned houses. All these things or facilities became possible, not because of ourselves, but because of many other people's direct or indirect involvement. Everything comes together. It is impossible to return to the way of life of a few centuries ago, when we depended on simple instruments, not all these machines. It is very clear to us that the facilities that we are enjoying now are the products of the activities of many people. In 24 hours

Left, A wall painting of White Manjughosha (Manjushri), the bodhisattva of wisdom, Tashikhyil Monastery.

you sleep on a bed – many people have been involved in that – and in the preparation of your food, too, especially for the non-vegetarian. Fame is definitely a product of other people – without the presence of other people the concept of fame would not even make sense. Also, the interest of Europe depends on America's interest and Western Europe's interest depends on the Eastern European economic situation. Each continent is heavily dependent on the others; that is the reality. Thus many of the things that we desire, such as wealth, fame and so forth, could not come into being without the active or indirect participation and co-operation of many other people.

Therefore, since we all have an equal right to be happy and since we are all linked to one another, no matter how important an individual is, logically the interest of the other five billion people on the planet is more important than that of one single person. By thinking along these lines, you can eventually develop a sense of global responsibility. Modern environmental problems, such as the depletion of the ozone layer, also clearly show us the need for world co-operation. It seems that with development, the whole world has become much smaller, but the human consciousness is still lagging behind.

This is not a question of religious practice, but a question of the future of humanity. This kind of wider or more altruistic attitude is very relevant in today's world. If we look at the situation from various angles, such as the complexity and inter-connectedness of the nature of modern existence, then we will gradually notice a change in our outlook, so that when we say "others" and when we think of others, we will no longer dismiss them as irrelevant to us. We will no longer feel indifferent.

Right, A man prostrating before a rock-face at the base of Chagpori Hill, which is adorned with hundreds of Buddhist deities, Lhasa, Tibet.

"If any individual is compassionate and altruistic, wherever that person moves, he or she will immediately make friends."

If you think only of yourself, if you forget the rights and well-being of others, or, worse still, if you exploit others, ultimately you will lose. You will have no friends who will show concern for your well-being. Moreover, if a tragedy befalls you, instead of feeling concerned, others might even secretly rejoice. By contrast, if an individual is compassionate and altruistic, and has the interests of others in mind, then irrespective of whether that person knows a lot of people, wherever that person moves, he or she will immediately make friends. And when that person faces a tragedy, there will be plenty of people who will come to help.

A true friendship develops on the basis of genuine human affection, not money or power. Of course, due to your power or wealth, more people may approach you with big smiles or gifts. But deep down these are not real friends of yours; these are friends of your wealth or power. As long as your fortune remains, then these people will often approach you. But when your fortunes decline, they will no longer be there. With this type of friend, nobody will make a sincere effort to help you if you need it. That is the reality.

Genuine human friendship is on the basis of human affection, irrespective of your position. Therefore, the more you show concern about the welfare and rights of others, the more you are a genuine friend. The more you remain open and sincere, then ultimately more benefits will come to you. If you forget or do not bother about others, then eventually you will lose your own benefit. So sometimes I tell people, if we really are selfish, then wise selfishness is much better than the selfishness of ignorance and narrow-mindedness.

Left, A monk walking along the roof of Sakya Monastery, Tibet.

For Buddhist practitioners, the development of wisdom is also very important – and here I mean wisdom which realizes Shunya, the ultimate nature of reality. The realization of Shunya gives you at least some kind of positive sense about cessation. Once you have some kind of feeling for the possibility of cessation, then it becomes clear that suffering is not final and that there is an alternative. If there is an alternative, then it is worth making an effort. If only two of the Buddha's Four Noble Truths exist - suffering and the cause of suffering -then there is not much meaning. But the other two Noble Truths, including cessation, point toward an alternative way of existence. There is a possibility of ending suffering. So it is worthwhile to realize the nature of suffering. Therefore wisdom is extremely important in increasing compassion infinitely.

So that is how one engages in the practice of Buddhism: there is an application of the faculty of wisdom, using intelligence, and an understanding of the nature of reality, together with the skilful means of generating compassion. I think that in your daily lives and in all sorts of your professional work, you can use this compassionate motivation.

Of course, in the field of education, there is no doubt that compassionate motivation is important and relevant. Irrespective of whether you are a believer or non-believer, compassion for the students' lives or futures, not only for their examinations, makes your work as a teacher much more effective. With that motivation, I think your students will remember you for the whole of their lives.

Similarly, in the field of health, there is an expression in Tibetan which says that the effectiveness of the treatment depends on how warm-hearted the physician is. Because of this

Left, A senior monk holding a ritual vase containing the gathered sand from the Kalachakra Mandala, Ki Monastery, Spiti, India.

expression, when treatments from a certain doctor do not work, people blame the doctor's character, speculating that perhaps that he or she was not a kind person. The poor doctor sometimes gets a very bad name! So in the medical field there is no doubt that compassionate motivation is something very relevant.

I think this is also the case with lawyers and politicians. If politicians and lawyers had more compassionate motivation then there would be less scandal. And as a result the whole community would get more peace. I think the work of politics would become more effective and more respected.

Finally, in my view, the worst thing is warfare. But even warfare with human affection and with human compassion is much less destructive. The completely mechanized warfare that is without human feeling is worse.

*Left, Monks at dawn on the roof of
Nechung Monastery.*

"Human compassion, or what I sometimes call 'human affection,' is the key factor for all human business."

Also, I think compassion and a sense of responsibility can also enter into the fields of science and engineering. Of course, from a purely scientific point of view, awful weapons such as nuclear bombs are remarkable achievements. But we can say that these are negative because they bring immense suffering to the world. Therefore, if we do not take into account human pain, human feelings, and human compassion, there is no demarcation between right and wrong. Therefore, human compassion can reach everywhere.

I find it a little bit difficult to apply this principle of compassion to the field of economics. But economists are human beings and of course they also need human affection, without which they would suffer. However, if you think only of profit, irrespective of the consequences, then drug dealers are not wrong, because, from the economic viewpoint, they are also making tremendous profits. But because this is very harmful for society and for the community, we call this wrong and name these people criminals. If that is the case, then I think arms dealers are in the same category. The arms trade is equally dangerous and irresponsible.

So I think for these reasons, human compassion, or what I sometimes call "human affection," is the key factor for all human business. Just as you see that with the palm of our hand all five fingers become useful, if these fingers were not connected to the palm they would be useless. Similarly, every human action that is without human feeling becomes

Right, Bundles of prayer flags and long rolls of printed mantras on sale at the Barkhor Market in front of the Jokhang Temple, Lhasa, Tibet.

dangerous. With human feeling and an appreciation of human values, all human activities become constructive.

Even religion, which is supposedly good for humanity, can become foul without that basic human compassionate attitude. Unfortunately even now there are problems which are entirely down to different religions. So human compassion is something fundamental. If that is there, then all other human activities become more useful.

Generally speaking, I have the impression that in education and some other areas there is some neglect of the issue of human motivation. Perhaps in ancient times religion was supposed to carry this responsibility. But now in the community, religion generally seems a little bit old-fashioned, so people are losing interest in it and in deeper human values. However, I think these should be two separate things. If you have respect for or interest in religion, that

is good. But even if you have no interest in religion, you should not forget the importance of these deeper human values.

There are various positive side-effects of enhancing one's feeling of compassion. One of them is that the greater the force of your compassion, the greater your resilience in confronting hardships and your ability to transform them into more positive conditions. One form of practice that seems to be quite effective is found in *A Guide to the Bodhisattva Way of Life*, a classic Buddhist text. In this practice you visualize your old self, the embodiment of self-centerdness, selfishness and so on, and then visualize a group of people who represent the masses of other sentient beings. Then you adopt a third person's point of view as a neutral, unbiased observer and make a comparative assessment of the value, the interests, and then the importance of these two groups. Also try to reflect upon the faults of being totally oblivious

Left, A monk performs a sacred dance, Tashikhyil Monastery.

to the well-being of other sentient beings and so on, and what this old self has really achieved as a result of leading such a way of life. Then reflect on the other sentient beings and see how important their well-being is, the need to serve them and so forth, and see what you, as a third neutral observer, would conclude as to whose interests and well-being are more important. You would naturally begin to feel more inclined toward the countless others.

I also think that the greater the force of your altruistic attitude toward sentient beings, the more courageous you become. The greater your courage, the less you feel prone to discouragement and loss of hope. Therefore, compassion is also a source of inner strength. With increased inner strength it is possible to develop firm determination and with determination there is a greater chance of success, no matter what obstacles there may be. On the other hand, if you feel hesitation, fear, and a lack of self-confidence, then often you will

Left, His Holiness the Dalai Lama at the Kalachakra Initiation, Spiti, India, August 2000.
Above, Freshly printed pages for prayer books, Ganden Monastery, Tibet.

"Every religion teaches the same message: be a warm-hearted person. They all emphasize compassion and forgiveness."

develop a pessimistic attitude. I consider that to be the real seed of failure. With a pessimistic attitude you cannot accomplish even something you could easily achieve. Whereas even if something is difficult to achieve, if you have an unshakeable determination there is eventually the possibility of achievement. Therefore, even in the conventional sense, compassion is very important for a successful future.

As I pointed out earlier, depending on the level of your wisdom, there are different levels of compassion, such as compassion which is motivated by genuine insight into the ultimate nature of reality, compassion which is motivated by the appreciation of the impermanent nature of existence, and compassion which is motivated by awareness of the suffering of other sentient beings. The level of your wisdom, or the depth of your insight into the nature of reality, determines the level of compassion that you will experience. From the Buddhist viewpoint, compassion with wisdom

is very essential. It is as if compassion is like a very honest person and wisdom is like a very able person – if you join these two, then the result is something very effective.

I see compassion, love, and forgiveness as common ground for all different religions, irrespective of tradition or philosophy. Although there are fundamental differences between different religious ideas, such as the acceptance of an Almighty Creator, every religion teaches us the same message: be a warm-hearted person. All of them emphasize the importance of compassion and forgiveness. Now in ancient times when the various religions were based in different places and there was less communication between them, there was no need for pluralism among the various religious traditions. But today, the world has become much smaller, so communication between different religious faiths has become very strong. Under such circumstances, I think pluralism among religious believers is very essential. Once you

Above, Samding monastery in the late afternoon light as seen from Nakartse, Tibet.

see the value to humanity through the centuries of these different religions through unbiased, objective study then there is plenty of reason to accept or to respect all these different religions. After all, in humanity there are so many different mental dispositions, that simply one religion, no matter how profound, cannot satisfy all the variety of people.

For instance, now, in spite of such a diversity of religious traditions, the majority of people still remain unattracted by religion. Of the five billion people, I believe only around one billion are true religious believers. While many people say, "My family background is Christian, Muslim or Buddhist, so I'm a Christian, Muslim or Buddhist," true believers, in their daily lives and particularly when some difficult situation arises, realize that they are followers of a particular religion. For example, I mean those who say, "I am Christian," and during that moment remember God, pray to God, and do not let out negative emotions. Of these true believers, I think there are perhaps less than one billion. The rest of humanity, four billion people, remain in the true sense non-believers. So one religion obviously cannot satisfy all of humanity. Under such circumstances, a variety of religions is actually necessary and useful, and therefore the only sensible thing is that all different religions work together and live harmoniously, helping one another. There have been positive developments recently and I have noticed closer relations forming between various religions.

So, having reflected upon the faults of a self-centered way of thinking and life, and also having reflected upon the positive consequences of being mindful of the well-being of other sentient beings and working for their benefit, and being convinced of this, then in

Left, A procession of monks with a statue of Maitreya, the Buddha of the future, on the final day of the Monlam prayer festival, Tashikhyil Monastery, Amdo, Eastern Tibet.

"You should remember that these mental transformations take time and are not easy."

Buddhist meditation there is a special training which is known as "the practice of Giving and Taking." This is especially designed to enhance your power of compassion and love toward other sentient beings. It basically involves visualizing taking upon yourself all the suffering, pain, negativity, and undesirable experiences of other sentient beings. You imagine taking these upon yourself and then giving away or sharing with others your own positive qualities, such as your virtuous states of mind, your positive energy, your wealth, your happiness, and so forth. Such a form of training, though it cannot actually result in a reduction of suffering by other sentient beings or a production of your own positive qualities, psychologically brings about a transformation in your mind so effectively that your feeling of love and compassion is much more enhanced.

Trying to implement this practice in your daily life is quite powerful and can be a very positive influence on your mind and on your health. If you feel that it seems worthwhile to practice, then irrespective of whether you are a believer or a non-believer, you should try to promote these basic human good qualities.

One thing you should remember is that these mental transformations take time and are not easy. I think some people from the West, where technology is so good, think that everything is automatic. You should not expect this spiritual transformation to take place within a short period; that is impossible. Keep it in your mind and make a constant effort, then after 1 year, 5 years, 10 years, 15 years, you will eventually find some change. I still sometimes find it very difficult to practice these things. However, I really do believe that these practices are extremely useful.

My favourite quotation from Shantideva's book is: "So long as sentient beings remain, so long as space remains, I will remain in order to serve, or in order to make some small contribution for the benefit of others."

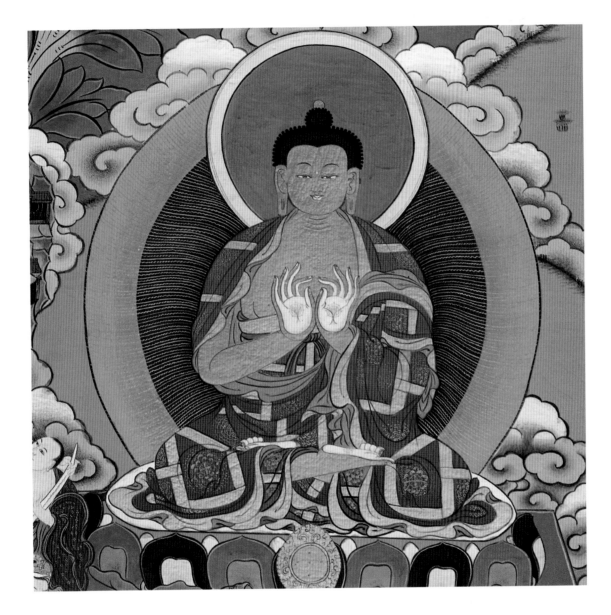

Above, A wall painting of Shakyamuni Buddha making the mudra of explaining the teachings,
Tashikhyil Monastery.

Interdependence,
Inter-connectedness
and the
Nature of Reality

Left, A monk playing a Tibetan singing bowl.

Above, Monks playing musical instruments at a ceremony at Tashikhyil Monastery, Amdo, Eastern Tibet.

"If we look at internal experiences, the past is no longer there and the future has not yet come: there is only the present."

In a discussion of interdependence, interconnectedness, and the nature of reality, the first question is: what is time? We cannot identify time as some sort of independent entity. Generally speaking, there are external matters and internal feelings or experiences. If we look at the external things, then generally there is the past, the present and the future. Yet if we look closely at "the present," such as the year, the month, the day, the hour, the minute, the second, we cannot find it. Just one second before the present is the past; and one second after is the future. There is no present. If there is no present, then it is difficult to talk about the past and the future, since both depend on the present. So if we look at external matters, it would seem that the past is just in our memory and the future is just in our imagination, nothing more than a vision.

But if we look at our internal experiences or states of consciousness, the past is no longer there and the future has not yet come: there is only the present. So things become somewhat complicated when we think along these lines. This is the nature of interdependency, the Sanskrit word *pratityasamutpada*. This is a very useful idea and it is one of my favorite subjects.

There are two levels of interdependence: a conventional level and a deeper level. First I will deal with the conventional level. When we speak of the Buddhist principle of interdependence, which is often referred to as "interdependent origination," we must bear in mind that there are many different levels of understanding of that principle. The more superficial level of understanding of the principle is the interdependent nature or relationship between cause and effect. The deeper level of understanding of the principle is much more pervasive and, in fact, encompasses the entire spectrum of reality. The principle of interdependent origination in relation to cause and effect states that nothing can come about without the corresponding causes and conditions;

everything comes into being as a result of an aggregation of causes and conditions.

If we consider the law of nature, we see it is not created by karma or by Buddha, it is just nature. We consider that Buddhahood developed according to natural law. Therefore, our experiences of pain and suffering, pleasure and joy, depend entirely on their own causes and conditions. Because of this natural relationship between causes and their effects, the Buddhist principle states that the less you desire a particular experience, event or phenomenon, the more effort you must put into preventing the aggregation of its causes and conditions, so that you can prevent the occurrence of that event. And the more you desire a particular event, outcome or experience, the more attention you must pay to ensure that these causes and conditions are accumulated so that you can enjoy the outcome.

I personally believe that the relationship between a cause and an effect is also a sort of natural law. I don't think that one could come up with a rational explanation as to why effects necessarily follow concordant causes and conditions. For instance, it is stated that afflictive emotional states like anger and hatred lead to undesirable consequences and, according to the Buddhist scriptures, one consequence of hatred and anger is ugliness. But there is not a full, rational account as to how ugliness is a consequence of that particular afflictive emotion. Yet in a way one can understand it, because when you experience very intense anger or hatred, even your facial expression changes and you assume a very ugly face. Similarly, there are certain types of mental and cognitive emotional states which bring about almost instantaneous positive changes in your facial expression. These states bring you presence of mind,

Right, His Holiness the Fourteenth Dalai Lama at a public teaching
London, England, 1999.

calmness, and serenity, and such an emotional state or thought could lead to a more desirable outcome. So one can see a type of connection, but not a full rational explanation.

But one might feel that there are certain types of emotional states, such as a very deep level of compassion, which are positive, yet, when they occur within your mind, one might say that at that particular instant there is no joy. For instance, a person may be fully under the influence of compassion and therefore sharing the suffering of the object of compassion. In that case, one could argue, from what I have said earlier, that compassion cannot be said to be a positive cause. But here I think one must understand that, while it is true that as a result of compassion, because one is fully engaged in sharing the suffering of the object of compassion, at that instant there is a certain degree of pain, this is very different from a pain which is being suffered by someone who is depressed, desperate, and helpless, and feels a loss of hope. In the case of compassionate suffering, although the person is undergoing a sort of pain, there is definitely a high degree of alertness, and there is no loss of control because the person is, in a way, willingly taking on the suffering of the other person. So on the surface these emotional states might look as though they have a similar outcome, but they are entirely different. In one case, the suffering is so overwhelming that the person has lost control and has given way to it, whereas in the case of compassion, the person is still in control of his or her thought.

Above, A monk walking past the entrance to a prayer hall of Drepung Monastery, Tibet.
Left, Monks at Drepung Monastery gazing out at the Himalayas.

*Above, Ritual weapons, which symbolize the powers of the protective deities, are stacked beneath
a wall painting of Ling Gesar, the epic hero of Tibetan Warriors, Tashikhyil Monastery.*

"If you understand the interdependent relationship between cause and effect, you will appreciate the Four Noble Truths."

Now if you understand the importance of appreciating the interdependent relationship between cause and effect, then you will appreciate the teachings on the Four Noble Truths. The entire teaching on the Four Noble Truths is based on the principle of causality. When the causal principle that is implied in these teachings is elaborated, you read Buddha's doctrine of the Twelve Links of Dependent Origination. In that teaching he stated that, because there is a particular cause, its effects follow; because the cause was created, the effect came about; and because there was ignorance, it led to action or karma.

So here you find three statements: one is that because the cause exists, the effect follows; because the cause was created, the effect was produced; and because there was ignorance, it led to the action. Now the first statement indicates that, from an affirmative point of view, when causes are aggregated, effects will naturally follow. And what is also implied in that statement is that it is due to the

mere aggregation of the causes and conditions that the effects come into being, and that, apart from the causal process, there is no external power or force such as a Creator and so forth which brings these things into being.

The second statement again points out another important characteristic of dependent origination, which is that the very cause which brings about the effects must itself have a cause. If the cause is an eternally existing, permanent absolute entity, then such an entity could not be itself an effect of something else. If that is the case, then it will not have the potential to produce an effect. Therefore, first of all there must be a cause; second, that very cause must itself have a cause.

And the third statement points out another important characteristic of the principle of dependent origination. It is that the effect must be commensurate with the cause – there must be a concordance between the two. Not just anything can produce anything; there must be a sort of special relationship between cause and effect. Buddha gave an example of ignorance leading to action. Here the implication is, "Who commits that action?" It is a sentient being – and by committing an act motivated by an ignorant state of mind, that being is in a way accumulating his or her own downfall. Since there is no living being that desires unhappiness or suffering, it is due to ignorance that the individual engages in an act which has the potential to produce undesirable consequences.

So we find that all the Twelve Links of Dependent Origination fall into three classes of phenomena. First, there are afflictive emotions and thoughts; second, there is the karmic action and its imprints; and third, there is its effect: suffering. So the principal message is that suffering is something that we all do not desire, but it is a consequence or an effect of ignorance. Buddha did not state that suffering is an effect of consciousness, because if that was the case, then the process of liberation or the process of purification would necessarily involve putting an end to the very continuum of consciousness. One moral that we can draw from this teaching is that the sufferings which are rooted in afflictive and negative emotions and thoughts can be removed. This ignorant state of mind can be dispelled, because we can generate insight which perceives the nature of reality. So we see that the principle of dependent origination shows how all these twelve links in the chain of dependent origination which forms an individual's entry into the cycle of existence are inter-connected.

Now if we were to apply this inter-connectedness to our perception of reality as a whole, then we could generate a great insight from it. For instance, we would then be able to appreciate the interdependent nature of one's own

Right, Pilgrims watch as monks perform a Sacred Cham dance, Tashikhyil Monastery, Amdo, Eastern Tibet.

"To have a happier future for oneself, you have to take care of everything that relates to you."

and others' interests: how the interests and well-being of human beings is dependent upon the well-being of animals living on the same planet. Similarly, if we develop such an understanding of the nature of reality, we would also be able to appreciate the inter-connectedness between the well-being of human beings and the natural environment. We could also consider the present, the future, and so forth. We would then be able to cultivate an outlook on reality which is very holistic and has very significant implications.

So in a few words, you can see that there are no independent causes of one's own happiness. It depends on many other factors. So the conclusion is that in order to have a happier future for oneself, you have to take care of everything that relates to you. That is, I think, quite a useful view.

So far, I have spoken about the principle of dependent origination from the perspective of the first level of understanding. We can see in the Buddhist scriptures the importance of understanding this level of the dependent origination. In fact, one of the Mahayana texts known as, *the Compendium of Deeds,* in which Shantideva quotes heavily from Buddha's sutras, points out the need to first of all appreciate the inter-connectedness of all events and phenomena: how, due to the causal and conditional process, phenomena and events come into being; and how crucial it is to respect that conventional reality, because it is at that level that we can understand how certain types of experiences lead to certain types of undesirable consequences, how certain causes, certain types of aggregation of

Left, A monk walking towards the monastery and town of Ganja, Amdo, Eastern Tibet.

causes and conditions can lead to more desirable consequences, and so forth; how, in fact, certain events can directly affect our well-being and experience. Because there is that sort of relationship, it is very crucial for practicing Buddhists to first develop a deep understanding of the perspective of the first level. Then Buddha states that one should go beyond that understanding and question the ultimate nature of the things that relate to each other in this inter-connected way. This points toward the Buddha's teachings on Emptiness.

In the teachings on the Twelve Links of Dependent Origination, the Buddha states that, although sentient beings do not desire suffering and dissatisfaction, it is through ignorance that they accumulate karmic actions which then lead to undesirable consequences. Now the question then is: what exactly is the nature of that ignorance? What is the mechanism that really leads an individual to act against what he or she fundamentally desires? Here Buddha points to the role of afflictive emotions and thoughts, like anger, hatred, attachment, and so forth, which blind the person's understanding of the nature of reality. If we were to examine the state of mind at the point when an individual experiences an intense emotion like hatred, anger or extreme attachment, we would find that, at that point, the person has a rather false notion of self: there is a kind of unquestioned assumption of an independently existing "I" or subject or person which is perceived, not necessarily consciously, as a kind of a master. It is not totally independent from the body or mind, nor is it to be identified with the body or mind, but there is something there which is somehow identified as the core of the being, the self, and there is a strong sort of grasping at that kind of identity or being. Based on that, you have strong emotional experiences, like attachment toward loved ones, or strong anger or hatred toward someone

Left, A lay woman spinning a prayer wheel, Tashikhyil Monastery, Amdo, Eastern Tibet.

"There is often a big disparity between the way in which we perceive things and the way things really are."

whom you perceive as threatening, and so forth.

Similarly, if we were to examine how we really perceive our object of desire or object of anger, we would notice that there is a kind of assumption of an independently existing entity, something which is worthy of being desired or worthy of being hated. Aside from the subtle perspective of the doctrine of Emptiness, even in our day-to-day lives we often find a disparity between the way we perceive things and the way things really exist. If that was not true, then the very idea of being deceived would not make sense. We often find ourselves totally disillusioned because we had false perceptions of reality. Once our illusion is dispelled, we realize that we have been deceived. So we often see in our own daily life cases where the appearance of something does not tally with the reality of the situation.

Similarly, as I pointed out in my talk on subtle impermanence, even from the perspective of the transient nature of phenomena there is often a big disparity between the way in which we perceive things and the way things really are. For instance, when we meet someone we say, "Oh, this is the very same person I've known for a long time." Again, when you see an object, you think, "Oh, this is the same object which I saw two days ago." This is a very crude way of talking about reality. What is actually happening here is a kind of a conflation between an image or a concept of an entity and the actual reality of the moment. In reality, the object or entity that we are perceiving has already gone through a lot of stages. It is dynamic, it is transient, it is momentary, so the object that we are perceiving

Right, Monks walking down a hill after the Kalachakra Initiation ceremony officiated by His Holiness the Dalai Lama, Ki Monastery, Spiti, India.

Above, A gathering of monks on the steps of the main prayer hall of Tashikhyil Monastery,
Amdo, Eastern Tibet.

"The object that we are perceiving now is never the same as the one which we perceived a day ago or two days ago."

now is never the same as the one which we perceived a day ago or two days ago, but we have the impression that we are perceiving the very same thing because what we are doing is conflating the concept of that object and the actual object. So we see again here a disparity between the way things appear to us and the way in which things really exist. Similarly, if we were to take the perspective of modern physics, then we would also find that there is a disparity between the common-sense view of reality and how scientists, from their point of view, would explain the nature of reality.

So what is clear from all this is the fact that there is some fault in our identification of an individual being as a self, as a person, or as an individual. But the question is: to what extent is it false? We cannot accept that the self or "I" does not exist at all, because if that is the case then a lot of our concerns, projects, and actions would not make any sense. Because of the fact that there is a self, our

concerns for attaining full liberation for the sake of other sentient beings, our concern for the well-being of other sentient beings, becomes very serious, because there is someone or something who would either suffer or benefit as a result of the stand we adopt or actions we engage in. So the question really is: to what extent is our notion of self, our sense of identity, our understanding of the being or individual, false or deceived, and to what extent is it correct? Making the demarcation between the correct view of the self and person and the false view of the self and person is extremely difficult. It is because of this difficulty – yet at the same time the importance of being able to make such a distinction – that there emerged in India various Buddhist philosophical schools. Some schools only accept "identitylessness" of persons, but not of external events or phenomena; some schools accept the "identitylessness" of not only persons but also of the whole of existence,

and even within that school there are various subtleties.

The reason why so much importance is placed on making the distinction is because it is so crucial to our attempt to liberate ourselves from suffering and its causes. This in part answers one of the questions that arose in one of the previous talks, that, if Buddhism accepts the doctrine of "no-self," what is it that takes rebirth?

We know that the doctrine of no-self or *anatman* is common to all the Buddhist schools of thought. The common doctrine of no-self is understood in terms of the denial of an independent and permanent self or soul. But what I will be presenting here is the understanding of Nagarjuna, as interpreted by the Indian pandit Chandrakirti. Nagarjuna, in his principal philosophical work, *The Fundamental Treatise on the Middle Way*, states that it is ignorance or misapprehension of the nature of reality which is at

*Left, Monks wait on a hillside as a giant
thangkha is carried through Sertang
Monastery ready to be unfurled at dawn,
Tagtsang Lhamo, Amdo, Eastern Tibet.*

149

the root of our suffering. The manner in which one can attain liberation from suffering is by dispelling this ignorant state of mind, this misconceived notion of reality, by generating insight into the ultimate nature of reality. Nagarjuna identifies two types of ignorance: one is grasping at an inherent or intrinsic reality of one's own self or being; the other is grasping at an inherent and independent existence of external events and things. He goes on to state that this grasping at a "self" or "I" comes about as a result of grasping at our aggregates: our body, mind, and mental functions. He further states that the fact that we have to dispel this ignorance from within our minds, that we have to see through the misconception of our misapprehension, is clear. But simply by distancing ourselves from that grasping, simply by thinking that it is false, simply by thinking that it is destructive, and so on cannot

ultimately help to free the individual from such forms of grasping. It is only by seeing through the illusion of that apprehension, it is only by generating an insight that would directly contradict the way in which, through that ignorance, we would normally perceive reality that we will be able to dispel that ignorance.

So how do we go about seeing through the illusion of this false notion of self? How do we generate the insight that would directly contradict that form of perception? Nagarjuna says that if a "self," "I," or person exists as we normally assume it to exist, if it exists as we falsely view it, then the more we look for it, the more we search for its essence, the referent behind our terms and labels, then the clearer it should become. But that is not the case. If we were to search for the self or person as we normally perceive it, then it disappears, it sort of disintegrates, and this is an indication that such a

Right, Monks walking past a large chorten (reliquary) at Sertang Monastery,
Tagtsang Lhamo, Amdo, Eastern Tibet.

Above, A young monk seated outside reading a prayer book, Samye Monastery, Tibet.

"An entity is composed of parts and there is a kind of necessary relationship between the whole and its parts."

notion of self was an illusion from the start. Because of this point, one of Nagarjuna's students, Aryadeva, stated in his *Four Hundred Verses on the Middle Way* that it is our ignorant conception or consciousness which is the seed of samsara (cyclic existence) and that things and events are its objects of grasping and apprehension. And it is only by seeing through the illusion of such a conception that we will be able to put an end to the process of existence.

We find in Nagarjuna's own writings extensive reasoning to refute the validity of our notion of self and negate the existence of self or person as we falsely perceive it. He argues that if the self or person is identical with the body, then just as the body is momentary, transient, changing every day, the self or the person should also be subject to the same law. For instance, a human being's bodily continuity can cease and, if the self is identical with the body, then the continuum of the self will also cease at that point. On the other hand, if

the self is totally independent of the body, then how can it make sense to say, when a person is physically ill, that the *person* is ill, and so forth? Therefore, apart from the interrelationships between various factors that form our being, there is no independent self.

Similarly, if we extend the same analysis to external reality, we find that, for example, every material object has directional parts, certain parts facing toward different directions. We know that so long as it is an entity it is composed of parts and that there is a kind of necessary relationship between the whole and its parts, so we find that apart from the interrelationship between the various parts and the idea of wholeness, there is no independent entity existing outside that interface. We can apply the same analysis to consciousness or mental phenomena. Here the only difference is that the characteristics of consciousness or mental phenomena are not material or physical. However, we can analyze this in terms of

the various instants or moments that form a continuum.

Since we cannot find the essence behind the label, or since we cannot find the referent behind the term, does it mean that nothing exists? The question could also be raised: is that absence of phenomena the meaning of the doctrine of Emptiness? Nagarjuna anticipates the criticism from the realists' perspective which argues that if phenomena do not exist as we perceive them, if phenomena cannot be found when we search for their essence, then they do not exist. Therefore, a person or self would not exist. And if a person does not exist, then there is no action or karma because the very idea of karma involves someone committing the act; and if there is no karma, then there cannot be suffering because there is no experiencer, then there is no cause. And if that is the case, there is no possibility of freedom from suffering because there is nothing from which to be freed. Furthermore, there is no path that would lead to that freedom. And if that is the case, there cannot be a spiritual community or sangha that would embark on the path toward that liberation. And if that is the case, then there is no possibility of a fully perfected being or Buddha. So the realists argue that if Nagarjuna's thesis is true, that the essence of things cannot be found, then nothing will exist and one will have to deny the existence of samsara and Nirvana and everything.

Nagarjuna says that such a criticism, that these consequences would follow from his thesis, indicates a lack of understanding of the subtle meaning of the doctrine of Emptiness, because the doctrine of Emptiness does not state or imply the non-existence of everything. Also the doctrine of Emptiness is not simply the thesis that things cannot be found when we search for their essence. The meaning of Emptiness is the interdependent nature of reality.

Left, A procession of monks playing musical instruments at a ceremony in Tashikhyil Monastery, Amdo, Eastern Tibet.

"The unfindability of phenomena when we search for their essence, indicates that phenomena lack intrinsic reality."

Nagarjuna goes on to say what he means by the claim that the true meaning of Emptiness emerges from an understanding of the principle of dependent origination. He states that because phenomena are dependent originations, because phenomena come about as a result of interdependent relationships between causes and conditions, they are empty. They are empty of inherent and independent status. An appreciation of that view is an understanding of the true Middle Way. In other words, when we understand dependent origination, we see that not only the existence of phenomena, but also the identity of phenomena, depend upon other factors.

So dependent origination can dispel extremes of both absolutism and nihilism, because the idea of "dependence" points toward a form of existence which lacks independent or absolute status, therefore it liberates the individual from extremes of absolutism. In addition, "origination" frees the individual from falling to the extremes of nihilism, because origination points toward an understanding of existence, that things do exist.

I stated earlier that the unfindability of phenomena or entities when we search for their essence is not really a full meaning of Emptiness, but at the same time it indicates that phenomena lack intrinsic reality, they lack independent and inherent existence. What is meant by this is that their existence and their identity are derived from mere interaction of various factors. Buddhapalita, one of the disciples of Nagarjuna, states that because phenomena come about due to the interaction

Right, A detail of a costume worn by a "gego" or discipline monk at a ceremony at Tashikhyil Monastery, Amdo, Eastern Tibet.

of various factors, their very existence and identity are derived from other factors. Otherwise, if they had independent existence, if they possessed intrinsic reality, then there would be no need for them to be dependent on other factors. The very fact that they depend on other factors is an indication that they lack independent or absolute status.

So the full understanding of Emptiness can come about only when one appreciates the subtlety of this principle of dependent origination – if one concludes that the ultimate nature is that phenomena cannot be found if we were to search for their essence. Nagarjuna states that if the principle or doctrine of Emptiness is not valid, if phenomena are not devoid of independent and inherent existence and intrinsic reality, then they will be absolute; therefore there will be no room for the principle of dependent origination to operate and there will be no room for the interdependent principle to operate. If that is the case, it would not be possible for causal principles to operate and therefore the holistic perception of reality also becomes a false notion. And if that is so, then the whole idea of the Four Noble Truths will be invalid because there is no causal principle operating. Then you will be denying the entire teachings of the Buddha.

In fact, what Nagarjuna does is to reverse all the criticisms levelled against his thesis, by stating that in the realists' position all the teachings of the Buddha would have to be denied. He sums up his criticism by saying that any system of belief or practice which denies the doctrine of Emptiness can explain nothing coherently, whereas any system of belief or thought which accepts this principle of interdependent origination, this doctrine of Emptiness, can come up with a coherent account of reality.

So what we find here is a very interesting

Left, Nuns perform a "kora" or circumambulation of Tashikhyil Monastery,
Amdo, Eastern Tibet.

"As your insight into the ultimate nature of reality is deepened, you will perceive phenomena as illusion-like."

complementary relationship between the two levels of understanding of dependent origination I spoke of earlier. The perspective of the first level really accounts for much of our everyday existence or everyday world of experience, where causes and conditions interact and there is a causal principle operating. That perspective of dependent origination, according to Buddhism, is called the correct view at the worldly level. The greater your appreciation of that perspective, the closer you will be able to come to the deeper level of understanding of dependent origination, because your understanding of the causal mechanism at that level is used to arrive at an understanding of the empty nature of all phenomena. Similarly, once your insight into the empty nature of all phenomena becomes deep, then your conviction in the efficacy of causes and effects will be strengthened, so there will be a greater respect for the conventional reality and the relative world. So there is a kind of interesting complementary relationship between the two perspectives.

As your insight into the ultimate nature of reality and Emptiness is deepened and enhanced, you will develop a perception of reality from which you will perceive phenomena and events as sort of illusory, illusion-like, and this mode of perceiving reality will permeate all your interactions with reality. Consequently, when you come across a situation in which you generate compassion, instead of becoming more detached from the object of compassion, your engagement will be deeper and fuller. This is because compassion is ultimately founded upon a valid mode of

Left, Prayer flags fluttering in the wind on the Pang La Pass with a view of Mount Everest in the background, Tibet.

thought and you will have gained a deeper insight into the nature of reality. Conversely, when you confront situations which would normally give rise to afflictive, negative emotions and responses on your part, there will be a certain degree of detachment and you will not fall prey to the influences of those negative and afflictive emotions. This is because, underlying those afflictive emotions and thoughts, such as desire, hatred, anger, and so forth, there is a mistaken notion of reality, which involves grasping at things as absolute, independent, and unitary. When you generate insight into Emptiness, the grip of these emotions on your mind will be loosened.

At the beginning of my talk I gave an example of our concept of time: ordinarily we presume there is a kind of an independent existent or independent entity called "time" present or past or future. But when we examine it at a deeper level, we find it is a mere convention.

Other than the interface between the three tenses, the present, future, and past, there is no such thing as an independently existing present moment, so we generate a sort of dynamic view of reality. Similarly, when I think of myself, although initially I might have an unquestioned assumption of there being an independent self, when I look closer I will find that, apart from the interface of various factors that constitute my being and various moments of the continuum that form my being, there is no such thing as an absolute independent entity. Since it is this mere conventional "self," "I" or person that goes toward the attainment of liberation or eventually transforms into Buddha, even Buddha is not absolute.

There is a similar case with the phenomenon mentioned earlier, the idea of Clear Light, which is the most subtle level of consciousness. Again, one should not conceive of it as some kind of independently existing entity.

Right, A senior lama presiding at a prayer ceremony, Tashikhyil Monastery, Amdo, Eastern Tibet.

Above, A "gego" or discipline monk watching over a prayer ceremony,
Tashikhyil Monastery, Amdo, Eastern Tibet.

"When we examine the nature of reality, we find it is empty of inherent existence."

Apart from the continuum of consciousness which forms this phenomenon called Clear Light, we cannot speak of an independently existing absolute entity.

Likewise, we will find that many of our concepts indicate a very deep, very complex interconnectedness. For instance, when we speak of ourselves as subjects, we can make sense of that notion only in relation to an object – the idea of a subject makes sense only in relation to an object. Similarly, the idea of action makes sense in relation to a being, an agent who commits the act. So if we were to analyze a lot of these concepts, we would find we cannot really separate the entity or the phenomenon from its context.

Again, if we go beyond the idea that things are mere designations or labels and ask whose conceptual thought creates the labels, whether it is the past conception or the future conception, whether it is the conception of a particular being or the collective conception, and so forth, we will not find an independent existence.

Even Emptiness itself, which is seen as the ultimate nature of reality, is not absolute, nor does it exist independently. We cannot conceive of Emptiness as independent of a basis of phenomena, because when we examine the nature of reality we find that it is empty of inherent existence. Then if we are to take that Emptiness itself as an object and look for its essence, again we will find that it is empty of inherent existence. Therefore Buddha taught the Emptiness of Emptiness. However, when we search for the true essence of a phenomenon or event, what we find is this Emptiness. But that does not mean that Emptiness itself is absolute, because Emptiness as a concept or as an entity cannot withstand this analysis. If we were to take Emptiness itself as an object and then again examine it, we cannot find it. However, in some scriptures we will find references to Emptiness as ultimate truth. Here one should understand what is the meaning of this term "ultimate." One should not mistake it in terms of Emptiness as being ultimately true, or absolute, but rather it is called "ultimate truth" because it is an object of the insight that has penetrated into the nature of reality.

The Challange for Humanity: An Interfaith Address

Left, A hazy moon over the Himalayas, India.

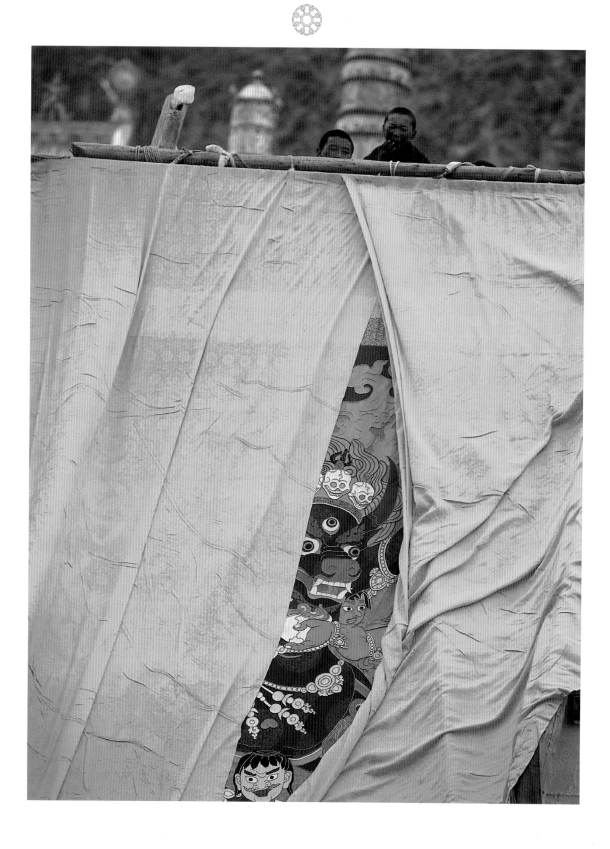

We have seen in this present age tremendous advances in the field of material development. As a result, there has been a marked improvement in the lives of human beings. Yet, at the same time, we are also aware that material development alone cannot answer all of humanity's dreams. Moreover, as material development reaches a higher and higher stage, we sometimes find that it brings with it certain complications, including more problems and challenges for us. Because of this fact, I think that all the major religious traditions of the world have the potential to contribute to the benefit and well-being of humanity, and also that they retain their relevance in the modern age.

However, since many of these major world religions evolved a long time ago in human history, I am quite sure that many aspects of their religious teachings and traditions reflect the needs and concerns of different times and cultures. Therefore, I think it is quite important to be able to make a distinction between what I call the "core" and "essence" of religious teachings and the cultural aspects of the particular tradition. What I would call the "essence" or "core" of religious traditions are the basic religious messages, such as the principles of love, compassion, and so forth, which always retain their relevance and importance, irrespective of time and circumstances. But as time changes, the cultural context changes, and I think it is important for the followers of religious traditions to be able to make the necessary changes that would reflect the particular concerns of their time and culture.

I think the most important task of any religious practitioner is to examine oneself within one's own mind and try to transform one's body, speech, and mind, and act according to

Left, Young monks above a large thangka of Yama Dharmaraja, the black buffalo-headed "Lord of the Dead", Tashikhyil Monastery.

"If one's faith remains only at the intellectual level, then I think that is a grave mistake."

the teachings and the principles of the religious tradition that one is following. This is very important. Conversely, if one's faith or practice of religion remains only at the intellectual level of knowledge, such as being familiar with certain doctrines without translating them into one's behavior or conduct, then I think that is a grave mistake. In fact, if someone possesses certain intellectual knowledge of religious traditions or teachings, yet his or her consciousness and mental continuum remain totally uninfluenced by it, then this could be quite destructive. It could lead to a situation in which the person, because of having the knowledge of the religious beliefs, could use the religion for the purposes of exploitation and manipulation. So, I think, as practitioners, our first responsibility is to watch ourselves.

The situation of today's world is completely different from the past. In the past, human communities and societies remained more or less independent of one another. Under such circumstances, ideas of a single religion, a monolithic culture, and so forth, made sense and had a place in the cultural context. But this situation has now completely changed as a result of various factors: easy access between various countries, an information revolution, easy transportation, and so forth. So human society can no longer function on that model.

Let us take as an example the city of London. London is a city which is multi-cultural and has multiple religions. Therefore, if we don't exercise caution and utilize our intelligence, there is a possibility of conflict based on divergent religious beliefs and cultures. So it is very important to have an outlook that takes into account the existence of multiple religions, the plurality of religions. The best way to meet this challenge is not just to study other religious traditions through reading books, but more importantly to meet with people from other religious traditions so that you can share experiences with them and learn from their experiences. Through

Above, Young monks at a ceremony at Tashikhyil Monastery, Amdo, Eastern Tibet.

personal contact you will be able to really appreciate the value of other religious traditions.

From a wider perspective, there are definitely strong grounds for appreciating pluralism in religion and culture, particularly in religion. It is a fact that among humanity there are many diverse mental dispositions, interests, needs, and so on. Therefore, the greater the diversity of religious traditions that are available, the greater their capacity to meet the needs of different people.

In the history of humanity there have been very tragic events which came about because of religion. Even to this day, we see that conflicts arise in the name of religion and the human community is further divided. If we were to meet this challenge, then I am sure we would find that there are enough grounds on which we can build harmony between the various religions and develop a genuine respect toward each other.

Another important challenge facing humanity now is the issue of environmental protection. In fact, a number of prominent environmentalists have expressed their wish to see more active initiatives taken by the different religious traditions and especially by their leaders. I think this is a wish that is very valid. Personally, I feel that much of the environmental problem really stems from our insatiable desire, lack of contentment, and greed. It is in the religious teachings that we find various instructions that enable us to keep a check on our desires and greed, and to positively transform our behavior and conduct. Therefore, I think religious traditions have not only a potential but also a great responsibility to make contributions in that direction.

Another thing that I consider very important, and which is a responsibility that religious traditions must take upon themselves, is the

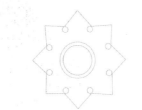

Left, A statue of Tsongkhapa in the chapel of the "gradual path to liberation" (Lamrim), the Potala Palace, Lhasa, Tibet.

"Voicing one's opposition to war alone is not enough. We must do something to bring about an end to war."

putting forward of a united front against war and conflict. I know that in human history there have been a few cases where, through war, freedom has been won and certain goals have been achieved. But I personally believe that war cannot ever lead to the ultimate solution of a problem. Therefore, I think it is important for all the religious traditions to take a united stand and voice their opposition to the very idea of war. But voicing one's opposition to war alone is not enough. We must do something to bring about an end to war and conflict, and one of the things that we have to seriously think about is the question of disarmament. I know that the motivating factor which triggers the need for weapons is human emotion – hatred and anger. But there is no way that we can completely eliminate anger and hatred from the minds of human beings. We can definitely reduce their force and alleviate them, but not completely eliminate them. That means that we have to make serious efforts to achieve disarmament.

Another challenge that we face is the question of population. I know that from the point of view of all religious traditions, life, human life in particular, is precious. From the viewpoint of individual human beings, the more humans there are the better it is, because then we have the opportunity for more human lives to come into being. However, if we look at this issue from a global perspective, then I think there is definitely a need for all religious traditions to give the population issue very serious thought, because the world's resources are limited. There is only a certain degree to which world resources can sustain human beings on this planet.

Left, Monks on their way to a ceremony before dawn at Sertang Monastery, Tagtsang Lhamo, Amdo, Eastern Tibet.

Above, Silhouette of His Holiness the Dalai Lama, Ki Monastery, Spiti, India.

Connolly